Under the Black Umbrella

Under the Black Umbrella

VOICES FROM COLONIAL KOREA, 1910–1945

HILDI KANG

Cornell University Press

Ithaca & London

First published 2001 by Cornell University Press
First printing, Cornell Paperbacks, 2005

Printed in the United States of America

Library of Congress Cataloging-in-Publication Data

Kang, Hildegarde S., 1934–
Under the black umbrella : voices from colonial
Korea, 1910–1945 / Hildi Kang.
p. cm.
Includes bibliographical references and index.
ISBN-13: 978-0-8014-3854-7 (cloth : alk. paper)
ISBN-13: 978-0-8014-7270-1 (pbk. : alk. paper)
1. Korea—History—Japanese occupation, 1910–1945.
2. Korea—Social conditions—20th century.
3. Japan—Politics and government—1912–1945.
I. Title.
DS916.54.H33 2001

951.9'03—dc21   00-011299

1 3 5 7 9 Cloth printing 10 8 6 4 2
3 5 7 9 Paperback printing 10 8 6 4 2

For
my Honorable Father-in-law
Kang Byung Ju
who made me aware of the voices
and
the Korean elders
who shared their life stories
with apologies
to the many
whose equally powerful stories
we were not able to include.

The reason for writing
is to shelter something from death.

ANDRE GIDE

CONTENTS

PREFACE: COLLECTING THE INTERVIEWS

Under the Black Umbrella chronicles the changes in Korea during the first half of the twentieth century, before and during the years when Korea existed as a colony of Japan. The Japanese presence hovered like a cosmic umbrella above the peninsula, casting a shadow of distrust, uncertainty, and fear over every life and every action. The takeover, to a greater or lesser degree, blocked the light of world awareness and left the Korean people living in the shadow cast by their colonial rulers.

My own knowledge of the Imperial Japanese colony originally came from two genres—the systematic detail in history books and the passionate stories of martyrs—and neither of these had prepared me for the gentle humor as my father-in-law recounted his early life. The family chuckled as father recalled entering a modern school dressed in old-fashioned *hanbok* (traditional Korean clothing), and smiled as he remembered helping his family make noodles by standing on the handles of their old noodle press. I let his stories slip by one after the other, until suddenly it struck me that every story took place under Japan's onerous rule of the peninsula. Where were the atrocities I had come to expect?

His memories shook loose my narrow view of colonial life and made me aware that often, under that shade cast by the Japanese presence, some people, some of the time, led close to normal lives. Of course, I now realized, during those years there must have been the entire gamut of life experiences, but where were their voices?

I looked again at the available sources, and still found only the catalogue of events. It is inevitable that over time, powerful personal events gradually become impersonal facts and detach from the lives that generated them. However, these events did once live and breathe as real people, and it was those people I decided to find. I wanted to seek out the richness and complexities of life under Japanese rule by collecting oral histories from Koreans who had lived through those times. Their stories became this book, restoring life to this period of Korean history, and shattering the silence long held by many who lived under the black umbrella of Japanese colonial rule.

Together, my husband and I developed our plan. We set out to interview not only a distinct ethnic group but also a narrow age range within that group, so we took care to think through the interview process, considering both what the older Koreans would deem respectful and what would put them most at ease. We knew that many, if not most, of these elders live within the cultural protection of the Korean community, rarely deal with Caucasians, and speak limited or no English. First we ruled out my typical western forthrightness, and planned that my husband, a native Korean speaker, would conduct the interviews.

He began by interviewing the most elderly Koreans in our San Francisco Bay area—first friends, then acquaintances, then those attending Korean senior centers. One by one, he traveled to each of the centers of the San Francisco Bay area and met with the presidents of the associations. After sharing tea and general conversation, he explained our project, presented his business card, and made clear his University of California affiliation. He left with an appointment to interview the president, and spent the next hour circulating and meeting individual elders. Then he returned week after week, tape recording interviews.

He began gently. Perhaps people would not want to bring forth old, possibly traumatic, memories—and at first people did hold back. "Oh," they said, "nothing much happened to me." Gradually, however, as they became used to this visitor and his tape recorder, individuals approached him saying, "You haven't heard my story yet," or "I have an interesting story to tell." Again and again he heard the comment, "I haven't talked about this in years," or "No one ever asked me that before." But memories returned quickly, and simple questions often released powerful stories.

In all interviews except one, the elders preferred to speak in their native Korean, and thus we had a second job at home. My husband translated the tapes into English, doing his best to catch the subtleties of Korean language with its different levels of speech. I typed the stories into the computer and puzzled over ways to organize and synthesize the thousand pages of material—what to include and what to leave out.

Inclusion began with one overarching goal—to document diversity. Stories were then excluded that fell into one of two categories—uneventful or redundant. Some people said that nothing much happened to them, and they were correct. Yet in their quiet lives there were often small moments of interest, and these entered the collection of smaller vignettes.

Next we sought to exclude redundancy. Many people shared similar experiences, especially at school or at work. From these, we chose the stories where details or personalities came through most strongly.

One single collection of stories cannot hope to capture the complete picture of life across an entire country, and our selection is admittedly limited by the locale from which we gathered our respondents—they are all people who wanted and could afford to move to America. The stories might take on a different tone if, for example, they had been gathered from among Koreans who had stayed in Korea, in North Korea, in Yanbyan, Manchuria, or from among those forced to labor in and still residing in Osaka, Japan.

In spite of this limitation, the stories presented here show lives that range from poverty to riches, and from comfort and acceptance to fear and torture. We are constantly reminded that even under the black cloud of Japanese rule, life was never one-dimensional.

The interviews in this book are arranged into six major stories and many small vignettes. We chose these six longer stories for the diversity of their experiences, and made no effort to reflect the percentage of poor, average, or well-to-do families. Yet looking at them now, we realize that of the six, two (Hong Ŭlsu and Chŏng Chaesu) started in severe poverty—one staying and the other rising by his own efforts; two (Kang Pyŏngju and Yu Hyegyŏng) came from prominent families and in spite of troubles, stayed there; and two (Yi Hajŏn and Yi Okhyŏn) were born into prominent families and pulled down by their troubles.

In all cases, to help jog their memories, we presented the elders with open-ended questions covering their town, schooling, jobs, religion, contact with Japanese authorities, and name change from Korean to Japanese. In addition, we encouraged them to relate any other experiences they remembered as significant in their lives. Taken together, the fifty men and women interviewed represented a wide range of occupations, education, birth locales, and religious beliefs.

This collection has three caveats. First, I acknowledge that these stories do not necessarily represent all Koreans; second, I acknowledge that not all memories may be completely accurate; and third, in a matter of semantics, I have not always translated the word *communist* as given us by the Korean elders.

First, with the exception of my father-in-law's memories taped years ago in Seoul, the interviews are from people living within a reasonable commute between Monterey and San Francisco, California. This may raise questions about the types of people most likely to emigrate, and whether their stories are skewed as a result. We found, however, that our local area was not restrictive, for over 100,000 Koreans now live in the greater San Francisco Bay area. The elders interviewed were both independent and dependent, educated and illiterate. They had been farmers, businesspeople, teachers, and scientists.

Second, memories are just that—memories. Each one is full of the passion of personal involvement. Many are clear and accurate, while others are colored by emotion or rumor. Throughout the book, small building blocks of historical information are supplied in an attempt to set these memories in context.

Beyond the scope of this book, but perhaps food for further discussion, are questions considering the veracity of remembered content, the effects of time and distance on memory, and the selectivity of geriatric reminiscences. Researchers with knowledge of colonization history may choose to consider whether or not the Korean situations are unique when compared with other colonized countries around the world.

Finally, in translating these memories, I have attempted to reserve the label *communist* for Communist Party members or their activities and to use the terms *leftist, radical,* or *partisan* in areas where actual membership in the party may not have existed. During the colonial years, various groups—leaning right, middle, and far left—worked to free Korea from Japan, and in that sense, all were nationalists. During the 1920s various communist groups entered Korea, all with the common goal of resistance to Japan. The current antagonism between Korean communists and nationalists emerged at the 1945 division of the peninsula into two countries, and from then on, the political groups polarized into "bad guys" and "good guys" (or reversed, from the northern point of view!).

In spite of these caveats and questions left unanswered, this book presents a fresh view of Korean history, told by the people whose lives, with both conscious effort and unconscious acceptance, intertwined the disparate themes of political oppression, economic gain, and personal passage from the ancient to the modern world. These elders graciously shared their memories with us and have given us a clear and varied picture of life under the black umbrella of the Japanese occupation. We offer them our thanks.

H. K.

Livermore, California

ACKNOWLEDGMENTS

The birth of a book depends on many people, and in this case, my first and greatest debt is to the more than fifty Korean elders who opened their hearts and memories and shared their stories with us. This book obviously could not exist without them.

In addition, numerous friends and acquaintances helped shape my chaotic thoughts into some semblance of order, and I am indebted to them all. The book had its genesis in my father-in-law's story; it grew to infancy during a conversation with Professor Gari Ledyard, who suggested this project and later read and critiqued the draft. The first tangible step, collecting the interviews, depended completely on the support and energy of my husband of over forty years, Sang Wook Kang, who gave uncountable hours to the task. Later, during the long hours of writing, his continual barrage of questions helped to focus my thoughts. Thanks also are due my sons, David C. and Steve Kang, for their constant encouragement and advice.

Special thanks go to attendees of the Fourth Pacific and Asian Conference on Korean Studies in Vancouver, whose lively response both tested and enriched my ideas. Professors Gi Wook Shin and Soon Won Park did me the honor of reading the draft and offering comments to guide the finished product, and Norman Thorpe contributed both suggestions and photographs from his extensive private collection. Assistance in locating other appropriate photographs came from Professor Hong Yung Lee and graduate assistant John Shin (University of California, Berkeley), and research assistants at the Library of Congress. Colleen Redpath restored and reproduced the private family photographs supplied by two of our interviewees.

On the technical side, I credit my daughter, editor Laura Kang Ward, with keeping me humble. After handing her what I thought was a flawless manuscript, ignoring her "All authors think their manuscripts are flawless" comment, I then saw red ink flow like a waterfall down the margin of every page. Thank you, Laura, for your amazing eye for detail.

Finally, my thanks to the outside reader who provided a wealth of useful comments and to Roger Haydon, my editor at Cornell University Press, for his years of interest and encouragement. From our first exploratory conversation, he has pushed me slowly from idea to reality.

CONVENTIONS USED

McCune-Reischauer System of Romanization

Not all Korean letters (*han'gŭl*) have clear and direct equivalents when transliterated into the roman alphabet, and thus Koreans commonly romanize their names to their own personal taste. For example, a single Korean name, Yi, may be spelled Lee, Li, Rhee, Rhi, Nee, or Ni. This book follows the McCune-Reischauer (M-R) system for all Korean words except those personal names where individuals have already chosen their own spelling. In this case, the M-R spelling comes first, followed by the personal spelling in brackets; for example, Hong Ŭlsu [Hong Eul Soo].

Pronunciation

vowels as follows:

a as in father	ae like the a in apple
ŏ as the u in but	o as in Ohio
e as in egg	oe like the ö in German
ŭ as the e in taken or spoken	u as in rule
i as in India	

consonants:

ch = j	t = d	t' = t	ch' = ch
p = b	k = g	k' = k	p' = p

Listing of Interviewees

Last name, first name [personal choice of spelling if there is one], (m) or (f) for male or female, birth date, job, province of birth.

Four interviewees chose to remain anonymous and are listed simply as last name, first initial [anonymous], (m) or (f), job.

Parentheses are used for interpolated translations;
for example, village school (*sŏdang*)
Brackets are used for explanatory material inserted
by the author into an interview.

Under the Black Umbrella

0 50 100 150 200 250 300 km

0 50 100 150 200 miles

RUSSIA

CHINA

N. HAMGYŎNG

Ch'ŏngjin

Kanggye

S. HAMGYŎNG

Chŏnch'ŏn

Sŏngjin

N. P'YŎNGAN

Sinŭiju

Hamhŭng

Chŏngju

S. P'YŎNGAN

Wŏnsan

EAST SEA
(SEA OF JAPAN)

P'yŏngyang

Sariwŏn

HWANGHAE

Kaesŏng

KANGWŎN

Seoul

Ullŭng-do

KYŎNGGI

Suwŏn

N. CH'UNGCH'ŎNG

S. CH'UNGCH'ŎNG

YELLOW SEA

Kongju

N. KYŎNGSANG

Taegu

N. CHŎLLA

S. KYŎNGSANG

Ulsan

Chinju

Masan

Kwangju

Pusan

S. CHŎLLA

KOREA STRAIT

JAPAN

Shimonoseki

Cheju Is.

Introduction

In the late 1800s, the people of Korea experienced a series of collisions with the modern world that sparked change of ever-increasing magnitude. These changes began before, and escalated during, the years of the Japanese occupation.

To glimpse the intensity of these changes, one must look back to see Korea before she arrived on the international scene. For hundreds of years the basic Korean lifestyle had been stable, with a population of subsistence farmers topped by a thin layer of educated elite.

A series of invasions (Mongols in 1231, Japanese in 1592, Manchus in 1627) caused Korea to close her borders to the entire world except Big Brother China. Not until the late 1800s, when traders, warriors, diplomats, and missionaries from around the world began forcing open the ports of eastern Asia, did Korea suddenly appear on the world scene.

Foreign observers thought Korea was hopelessly backward and incapable of bringing herself into the modern world, but these foreigners did not see the whole picture. Koreans already had taken sporadic steps toward internal reform, attempting to modernize while also preserving their identity.

An early religious reform known as *Tonghak* began in 1860. One interviewee tells how his father "was a preacher of *Tonghak*. This Eastern Learning rejected western things as defiling Korean tradition." By 1894 this sect became a full-fledged rebellion, as peasants struggled against both indigenous Korean injustices and increasing Japanese influence.[1]

The many *Kabo* Reforms followed in 1894, starting in the upper echelons of Korean power. These reforms attempted to reconstruct the government and abolish class distinctions. Koreans, however, never got the chance to continue their own reforms because the Japanese slowly and surely forced Korea under their control. Subsequently, from 1910 until 1945, Imperial Japan colonized the peninsula and became for Korea both oppressor and agent of change.

THE COLONIAL PERIODS

Japanese rule of Korea is generally divided into three periods. First came the dark age of *subjugation*, when the military ruled by threat and violence (1910–1919). After the Korean Independence Movement in March 1919, the Japanese eased into a time of *cultural accommodation* (1920–1931), allowing some freedoms in schools, newspapers, and businesses. Then came the years of *assimilation*, 1931–1945, with a renewed tightening of controls and forced participation in the Japanese war effort.

In spite of the difficulties, Japanese rule did bring material progress to Korea. The Japanese developed an infrastructure of roads, railroads, and harbors; modernized schools across the land; upgraded the administrative and judicial systems; and transformed the economy from agrarian to semi-industrial.

These changes, however, brought minimal joy to Koreans, for the real goal was to speed development in Japan and help the Japanese expansion effort. Koreans often ate Manchurian beans, millet, or barley instead of their usual rice, for, increasingly, the rice harvest got sent to Japan.[2] Pak Sŏngp'il remembers local farmers confronting the Japanese police and asking, "How can you expect us to survive, when you take away 70 percent of what we make!"

Rice wasn't the only commodity leaving Korea for Japan. Cotton growers produced 200 million pounds of cotton in 1939, but shipped 160 million pounds of it to Japan.[3] And although the Japanese in Korea accounted for only 2.5 percent of the population, they held more than 80 percent of all senior government posts.[4]

FROM DICHOTOMY TO COMPLEXITY

The occupation ended in 1945. The debate raged then, and continues to this day, over whether that occupation was beneficial or harmful for Korea. When elder Yi Sangdo recalled the Japanese-built dams and bridges that brought flood control to his village, he admitted, "I must say, their organ-

Introduction

ization impressed me. I think probably it was good, in the long run." But Yang Sŏngdŏk just as strongly insists, "They had sinister plans . . . to eliminate any vestiges of Korean consciousness."

Scholars echo the words of the elders. Carter Eckert looked at both sides of the picture: "If one finds [in the colonial period] enlightenment and progress, one also finds national subjugation, shame and betrayal, political authoritarianism and violence, and profound human suffering."[5] Bruce Cumings also stressed this dichotomy when he said that politically Koreans could barely breathe, but economically there was significant, if unevenly distributed, growth.[6] Other scholars have weighed in on one side or the other of colonial rule and examined backwardness versus progress, plunder versus development, imperial repression versus national resistance, and Japanese culture versus Korean culture.

These attempts to understand the occupation have pitted extremes against one another, but today, with continued academic research, dichotomies fade and complexities become ever more apparent. As Korea, by her own choice or by outside coercion, rushed forward into the modern world, life became a time of multiple possibilities.

Each aspect of colonial life affected the others, and all factors—from fear to peaceful coexistence—were at work at the same time. For some, life was hard. For others life was not so hard, and the difference depended on fragile changes in where one lived, or when, or even on the personality of a local police chief.

The confusion and chaos of those years has usually been attributed to the Japanese, but the possibility exists that at least some of it came as a natural by-product of the process of change itself.

Changes of all sorts impacted the lives of every elder we interviewed, whether those changes were large or small, embraced or rejected. Elder Hong Ŭlsu still feels guilt when he recalls stealing from his mother in order to get an education, and he speaks of wide-eyed amazement as he confronted the "huge, black monster" of his first train. Miss Yu Tŏkhŭi, on the other hand, noticed that events of the 1940s upset the social order of her entire village as servants and masters together were drafted into the army. "Everybody's fate was the same, so they all became equal. The old order crumbled."

Not everyone changes, of course, but a period of transition can be devastating even to those who resist, who hang on to tradition, for daily they see their personal security rattled by their renegade family members or neighbors. In several interviews we heard the stress caused by clutching tightly to tradition—"Our neighbors in the village would wag their fingers at us. 'What good is it to learn at the hand of the Japanese?' they asked," and again, "Grandfather took one look at me with my long braid cut off and went into a great rage. He yelled, 'You became Japanese. Do not step inside this gate.'"

DIVISIONS OF THIS BOOK

The divisions of this book roughly echo the divisions commonly attributed to the Japanese colonial period, but where the colonial years have three main divisions, this book has only two, Change by Choice and Change by Coercion.

The early colonial period, subjugation, is contained in chapter 1, a single chapter that reaches back before the colonial period into the late 1800s. This chapter in no way does justice to the early turmoil; it only hints at years that Kang Pyŏngju describes as a time when "cultural earthquakes rocked our country" and "the modern world knocked, pounded, and battered its way into our consciousness." In 1910, military changes eclipsed the cultural ones, as Japan took over the peninsula and began its period of military rule. A Japanese reporter for the *Tokyo Nichi Nichi Shinbun* commented in an editorial on October 2, 1910, "Newspapers were checked one by one; controls on companies were exercised to an extreme, unsatisfactory companies being destroyed one after the other. Reporters and writers were at their wit's end, gasping. If one grumbled, he would be arrested . . . I felt as if I were in hell."[7]

Those who were adults during this period are no longer with us, yet many of the interviewees began their own stories with, "First let me tell you about my father. He was one of the very first to . . ." become Christian, cut his long hair, go to western school, be an auto salesman.

Part I: Change by Choice (chapters 2–7) contains interviews whose action takes place during the years of cultural accommodation (1920–1931). It opens with the Independence Movement of March 1, 1919, for it was that outcry that forced the Japanese government to relax its tight hold. This part contains individual chapters on three elders born between 1905 and 1911, who for the most part lived their lives according to their own choice. Chapters of vignettes round out the picture of educational choices and business adventures. To help us remember that many choices came with a price, the section ends with the story of a young man who suffered jail, torture, and continual harassment for his choice of rather mild anti-Japanese activities.

Part II: Change by Coercion (chapters 8–14) sets forth stories that focus on the tightening grip of Japan during the assimilation years (1931–1945). It includes the individual chapters of three people born in the 1920s who reach adulthood as the war escalates. In general this was a time of intense coercion, yet, particularly in the chapters of short vignettes, we see the spaces left for individual choice.

The reader will notice that some lives are presented as full chapters, and some are reflected in vignettes on a topic. This system developed because many people, it turned out, lived ordinary lives. Interview after interview began with sentences such as, "Nothing much happened to me. The Japanese people were not bad. We got along. It was the police that bothered us. I just stayed out of their way." However, these same people had small bits of salt and pepper tucked away in their interviews that, when gathered together, added dimension to the larger picture.

These stories of life under the black umbrella of colonial rule cover the full gamut of emotions, as people faced changes both pleasant and difficult. The resilient human spirit, echoed in many of the interviews, is clearly expressed by Kang Pyŏngju as he concludes his own story. "The places we lived, though rural, were full of natural beauty. I look at these sojourns, paid for by the bank over the years, as free sightseeing tours. In that sense, it was not a wasted experience, but rather an opportunity."

1 : First Encounters

When Korea, long known as the Hermit Kingdom, opened its doors to the world, its people faced a dizzying barrage of first encounters. Businessmen, missionaries, soldiers, and statesmen from all corners of the world brought new inventions, languages, weapons, and rules. That first generation, those who were adults between 1880 and 1910, are the ones against whom the explosive crash of opposing ideas hit with unexpected force. They should tell this story, but they are no longer alive. Their children speak for them.

KANG PYŎNGJU [KANG BYUNG JU]
(m) b. 1910, bank manager, North P'yŏngan Province:
I want to tell you about my grandfather, Kang Chundal. He was born in 1850, during the reign of King Ch'ŏlchong, in our clan village to the east of Chŏngju city. Grandfather belonged to a long line of traditional village elders. He held strongly to that tradition and never ventured far from his village, but when the outside world shoved new ideas within his grasp, he was ready.

Grandfather's adult life was a time when cultural earthquakes rocked our country. The modern world knocked, pounded, and battered its way into our consciousness. Now remember, our northern part of the country had been settled centuries earlier by free thinkers who had fled or been exiled from the royal court.[1]

These people did pretty much as they pleased, and most actually welcomed these modern innovations. My grandfather made four major changes.

First, Grandfather became a Christian. Around 1895, already forty-five years old, he set out one day from our village to the neighboring city of

*Outside Seoul's Great South Gate (Namdaemun),
showing one of the early trolley cars. 1904
(Courtesy of the Library of Congress, LC-USZ62–72551)*

Chŏngju. His white robes and wide-brimmed hat blended in with all the others in the crowded city.

On this day a foreigner stood in the street talking about a new religion. The message intrigued him, and soon he became one of the first converts to Protestant Christianity. Can you imagine what it must have been like when he returned to his village? Since he was the patriarch, he just made everybody in our village change to Christianity, whether they liked it or not.

His next major change came in 1900, when he chose a name for his new daughter-in-law and added it to the *hojŏk* (local registry for citizens) which until then had listed women without their names, only "so-and-so's daughter." It happened like this. Grandfather's son (my father) was 13 when he got married that year. His young wife had no personal name and that didn't matter, because in Korean tradition we don't call people by their personal names, anyway.

However, when these children married, it was just after the *Kabo* Reforms of 1894–95, which included a new law saying women should be listed *by name* in the family's household register.[2] Most families ignored this, but our grandfather recognized another tradition he was ready to break.

Of course, in order to register the daughter-in-law, she had to have a name. Grandfather picked two syllables—most Korean names have two syllables. He chose one from his son's first name, Sŏhyŏng, and made up the other. Her name became Sŏyun.

Eight years later, he sent his son to school. A western-style school, Osan High School, had just opened in our area, teaching history, science, and mathematics instead of the Chinese classics.[3] Yi Sŭnghun, a Korean, started this boys' school, not the Japanese.

The school opened in 1907 and within a year Grandfather decided that his son should attend. Think of it. This school was brand new. There was no preparation for it. Any boy or man who qualified entered these first classes. So my father entered the school when he was twenty-one years old, eight years married, and a father himself.

Finally, in 1912 and sixty-two years old, Grandfather made his fourth and final break with tradition. He sent his only son away from the village to learn to be a doctor of western medicine, and so my father became one of the first to graduate from the Keijo Medical College. (In fact, just recently I received from Seoul a document commemorating his graduation.) When he finished his schooling, he returned to our village and opened a medical practice in nearby Napch'ŏn, about a twenty-minute walk away.

The story is that since Father had such good schooling, and had been married very young to a woman who had no schooling at all (the custom in those days), he was not happy living with her in the farm village. He told my mother to "just do what you want" with the property, and he went off to Manchuria to practice medicine and live his own life. After that, Mother ran the entire estate, and kept track of the tenant farmers.

Remember, the Manchurian border was very near to our village. I think Father returned to visit his family several times a year, because he had seven

First Encounters

children born between 1906 and 1928. These parents educated all seven children through both high school and college—all of us, three boys and four *girls*. This is amazing because it was still a time when girls rarely even went to high school.

Here is a story my father told from his time in Manchuria. A Manchurian warlord had heard that he could live forever if he ate the liver ripped out of a living person. One day Father was summoned to the warlord's headquarters.

"I hear that you are a western-style doctor. You can do surgery?"

"Yes, Your Honor."

"Three soldiers have been captured and are about to be executed. Before I kill them, while they are alive, you must choose one and cut out his liver." The warlord stared, waiting.

"No. I cannot do such a cruel thing," Father answered.

"Then I will execute you, also."

So Father did as he was told.

I remember one day when I was about five, so it must have been in 1915, Grandfather was putting a thatched roof on the pig pen behind the house and I was playing nearby. Suddenly, over the Sŏdang Hill, one of the hills surrounding our village, appeared Japanese military police in their shiny brown uniforms followed by their Korean aides.

In those days, Koreans weren't called policemen, but rather assistants. The colonial government wanted help securing the country to its own advantage so it recruited Korean men who could speak Japanese. It gave these men black uniforms and had them walk alongside the brown uniforms of the military police.

About a dozen of these arrogant fellows descended upon us, surrounded Grandfather, bound him with rope, and started to take him away. They didn't notice me. I hurried inside and told Mother. She ran out and pleaded with the police.

"What has my father-in-law done that you bind him and drag him away?"

She carried on, cried, pleaded, but they kicked her and took him away. We never knew the reason. He came back in a few days.

Here is a story that shows just how wealthy my Grandmother Kim's family was, and how tight they were with their money. It also shows how our troubles came, not just from the Japanese, but from our own men as well. After the Japanese occupation, many Koreans used guerrilla tactics to fight the Japanese. They called themselves the Independence Army. To pay for their fighting, they went around extorting money from wealthy people. They did not bother us Kangs at all, but they earmarked the Kims. The Kims were warned to get money ready, because the guerrillas would be back for it. The father of the family was so reluctant to part with money that when the army returned he wouldn't give them any, and right there, the soldiers killed him.

Yi Sangdo's father, on the other hand, rejected everything western and became a proponent of the new religious movement called Tonghak, or "Eastern Learning," which brought together elements from Confucianism, Buddhism, and Taoism, proclaimed equality for the peasants, the betterment of village conditions, and reform of the corrupt government.

YI SANGDO, (m) b. 1910, truck driver, Kyŏnggi Province:
I want to tell about my father. He was a preacher of *Ch'ŏndogyo, Tonghak*. This "Eastern Learning," very chauvinistic, rejected all western things as defiling Korean tradition.

Father did not get paid for preaching. My elder brothers supported him. The believers, instead of giving a cash offering, gave small units of rice depending upon how many members were in their family. This was sold and the money sent to Seoul to pay the expenses at the religion's headquarters.

People came to our large house to make plans for rallies. I remember meetings in our house—secret meetings. Once I heard grownups talking about a rally where they would cry out *"Mansei, Mansei"* (May Korea live ten thousand years).

Father hated the Japanese coming, but to me, they weren't all that bad. Whenever we had a rainy season, our village flooded. Look what happened: Those Japanese came and built reservoirs, dams, and bridges. One of the taxes had to be paid in rocks. Each family had to go out two or three times a year and find a certain amount of small rocks. They used these to build roads.

I must say their organization impressed me. They planned things. They came with blueprints. They built things that worked. The bridge they built in our village lasted through all the rains and flooding. They also brought little things—sharp razor blades, matches that caught fire quickly, the record player—I know that those came from Europe, so eventually we

First Encounters

would have gotten them. But the Japanese brought them first. I think probably it was good, in the long run.

The early Japanese policies were not kind to Korea. Japan stationed a large army in Korea, plus thousands of Japanese civil servants. The first governor, General Terauchi Masatake, put a stranglehold on Korean political and economic development. He prohibited meetings, closed newspapers, and ordered burned over 200,000 books containing information such as Korean history, Korean geography, and free-thinking modern ideas. A tight network of spies and informers worked alongside the police, and by 1918, over 200,000 Koreans had been labeled rebellious, arrested, and tortured.[4]

People were arrested, often with no idea of what was charged against them, and the most innocent act could bring unexpected repercussions. One gentleman told how his father's purchase of a cow brought the Japanese police. "'Where did you get the money?' they asked. 'You must have been spying.' He was then ordered to report to the police station every single morning at nine o'clock."

YI SŬNGBONG, (m) b. 1912, tailor, Kyŏnggi Province:
My uncle was a cavalry officer under the old Korean kingdom. When the Japanese took over, he had some problem because of his former military position. I was told not to talk about it. I think they didn't want me to know.

YI OKHYŎN, (f) b. 1911, housewife, North P'yŏngan Province:
Grandfather on my mother's side was an educated man, so knowledgeable in Chinese, I am told, that when the king of Korea sent a mission to China, my mother's father accompanied the mission as interpreter.

This grandfather, in order to avoid the war between Japan and Russia in 1904, moved to Ko'ŭp, a small village near the Manchurian border by the Yalu River. He bought up lots of land and settled there. We became a prominent family in the community, so that my father's elder brother, my first uncle, became *myŏnjang*, head of the township.

KIM WŎN'GŬK [KIM WON KEUK],
(m) b. 1918, Tobacco Authority officer, North Hamgyŏng Province:
My father was President of the Young Businessmen's Association in our area and one of the first modern Koreans to cut his hair short.

We owned one of the largest plots of land in the area, with about 20,000 p'yŏng [a *p'yŏng* is a unit of area about 6' × 6']. We had an orchard with 3,000 trees, and lots of potatoes, most of which were used to feed the pigs that we raised. We also raised rabbits and chickens. We fenced off part of the mountain behind the village and in that area we let loose about 500 chickens. The trees dropped leaves and seeds that made food for them, very nutritious, so they got fat quickly. We supplied chickens to the soldiers of the nineteenth Japanese infantry division stationed nearby in Nanam city.

To show you how modern Father was, instead of farming in the old way by hand, he ordered machinery from Japan for digging and weeding, and because of Father's connections with the government, every day we had visitors from the county government or the provincial government, all Japanese. When the local government wanted to train young people in agricultural methods, they sent the people to our house to learn from my father.

As part of the Young Businessmen's Association, in winter when it was too cold to farm, Father organized weaving projects using machines to make all sorts of things from the rice straw. They sold the products and used the profit for association activities.

The Japanese began a land survey and required land holders to register their holdings. The belief circulated that many peasants, through negligence or ignorance, failed to do so and had their land confiscated by the Governor-General, causing Koreans to label it the Japanese "land grab."

HONG ŬLSU [HONG EUL SOO],
(m) b. 1905, teacher/businessman, Yangsan, South Kyŏngsang Province:
When the Japanese took over, they instituted measuring each farm. They said the survey was conducted so that people could know exactly what they owned. All the land that went unclaimed, of course, the Japanese took for themselves.

One thing the Japanese did at this time was to record the ownership of each farm property, because before, Koreans had no documentation of ownership. For generations, Koreans just said so-and-so's rice field is next to so-and-so's.[5]

Some Koreans were clever, and when the engineers surveyed the land, these farmers pointed to some areas that did not belong to them and

First Encounters

claimed it for their own. When the surveying was done and recorded on a map, they ended up with farms larger than they had ever truly owned. The farmers who were ignorant lost out.

The Japanese also took much of the land for themselves. They did not bother with small plots in hilly places, but targeted for this extortion the fertile agricultural plains. Since they held power, they got away with enormous amounts of land this way.[6]

While most people adjusted to Japanese rule, some chose to fight, secretly crossing over into Manchuria to join the resistance. Several of our interviewees told of relatives who became volunteer freedom fighters. They walked and hid in the mountains, in pig pens and chicken coops, until they crossed over the Yalu River into Manchuria. Once there, they joined General Yi Tonghwi[7] and other resistance leaders collecting money, smuggling weapons from Siberia, and training soldiers. Some even set up schools for exiled Korean children. In addition, until repression became too severe, sporadic armed resistance took place right inside Korea.

CHIN MYŎNGHŬI, (f) b. 1932, housewife, South Hamgyŏng Province:
My grandfather contributed, around the turn of the century, to anti-Japanese activists inside Korea, so he took his family and fled for safety to Manchuria. Even that was not safe, so they kept going and ended up in Czarist Russia. Father was only seven, so he grew up there in Russia. His Russian is fluent. Grandfather died in Russia and in 1918, after the Russian revolution, my father returned to Korea.

CHŎNG T'AE'IK, (m) b. 1911, farmer, Kangwŏn Province:
My grandfather (mother's father) was one of the militia that fought to keep the Japanese out of Kyŏngsang Province, but we were defeated, you know.

About 1910 or 1911 many of Grandfather's comrades were caught and beheaded by the Japanese. To save himself, Grandfather disappeared. He just took off. He couldn't tell anybody, of course, because then the Japanese would follow him.

In those days, there were no highways, so he walked at night along mountain paths on the eastern coast. He ended up in Kangwŏn Province.

The farmers there are different from other Korean farmers. They burn the trees to clear the plot, plant one year, and then they move on. Only in the high mountains of Kangwŏn Province do they do this. They are a separate group of people, like a tribe. They stick to themselves.

Grandfather joined them to keep away from the Japanese police. Once he got established there—not settled, just established—he gradually sent for members of his family.

My own father couldn't make it as a farmer in his home village, so one day he just up and ran away. Several years later, we found that he had gone up in the mountains to join his wife's family. By moving around, they actually did all right. When I was about nine or ten, we all went with Father and lived there, off and on, for a long time.

As Japanese rule reached the end of its first decade, Koreans expressed increasing resentment and anger. Aided by the spread of literacy and communication, popular disturbances broke out one after another.

When the First World War ended, leaders of the Korean nationalist movement heard of President Woodrow Wilson's "doctrine of self-determination" and decided the time had come to take action. They planned to make a public proclamation of independence, and chose the date of March 1, 1919.

PART ONE

Change by Choice

OVERVIEW

The Korean Independence Movement, and the outside world's reaction to it, precipitated the first major shift in Japanese policy. The extent of the demonstrations surprised the Japanese, causing them to rethink and re- structure their rule. They returned to the Koreans a modicum of personal choice by deregulating some businesses and hiring a small percentage of Koreans into government jobs. Education expanded, and Korean-owned newspapers began publication.[1]

However, along with these areas of increased freedom came companion areas of tightened control, so that some historians have called it a time of "cosmetic changes" with strengthened police control, an expanded network of spies and informers, more prisons, and more arrests for ideological crimes.[2]

Whether or not the changes were superficial, they did benefit many Ko- reans. The following chapters, therefore, focus on this element of personal choice. Hong Ŭlsu was sixteen when he first saw a map of the world, and he chose education to propel himself into that world. Kang Pyŏngju chose to apply for one of the newly opened government positions and moved through the "eye of a needle" to become a bank manager. Yi Okhyŏn took advantage of new opportunities to apply for and received permission to study piano in Canada, but her fiancé's choice to teach the farmers put an end to both of their dreams. Vignettes from other lives, stories of personal choice related to education and vocation, round out this picture of a time filled with changes between the old and the new.

Pak Sŏng P'il's grandfather, mother, and sister, about 1917.
Grandfather was head of Kijang township, South Kyŏngsan province.
(Courtesy of Pak Sŏng P'il. Photo restored by Colleen Redpath)

2 : Shouts of Independence

MARCH 1, 1919

The Independence Movement began simply. Thirty-three representatives of the Korean people met at a restaurant in Seoul, read aloud their declaration, and formally proclaimed Korea to be an independent nation. Having made their public statement, the men walked to the Japanese police station and turned themselves in.

What happened next surprised everyone. Unplanned and unexpected, those who had been silent became vocal. Over the following months, thousands of students, shopkeepers, farmers, and others, both old and young, called out for freedom in separate demonstrations throughout the country.

The Japanese were stunned by the enormity of the movement and quickly moved to crush it by military force. Japanese records show 46,948 arrests, 7,509 killed, and 15,961 injured.[1] In one of the worst acts of cruelty, twenty-nine people were locked in a church that was then set afire; all inside burned to death.

KIM SUNOK, (m) b. 1910, peddler/fireman, Kyŏnggi Province:
Map'o was just a village over the hill from Seoul when I lived there, and the tram came all the way from Seoul to Map'o. One day when I was ten years old, I was playing near the tracks and I saw people in the tram. They wore Korean clothes but western hats. Those hats—they took them off and waved them in the air, screaming at the top of their lungs, "Independence now!"

I asked the grownups what was happening. They said they wanted to get their country back. Those people on the tram were going to Seoul to join a demonstration.

A friend and I decided to follow. We went up the hill and down the other side toward Seoul. As we got near an area where noblemen of the Chosŏn dynasty had their houses, we saw hundreds of Koreans coming toward us shouting that same shout, "Independence now!"

Men walked in front waving Korean flags. Behind them came a crowd, pushing, shoving, shouting, "*Mansei!*" (*Man* means 10,000; implied translation is "May Korea live ten thousand years.") My friend and I, looking for a good time, joined right in.

We came to a police station. We could look right in the window, and I saw a policeman inside lift the receiver off his phone. I figured he was telling his boss about the crowd outside. A fellow near me tossed a huge stick through that window. The policeman dropped the phone, ran into the inner room, and tried to hide under a blanket. He was really shaking with fear.

We moved on toward Seoul station, yelling and pushing. There is an overpass above the railroad, and when we got to it we saw—right in front of us—Japanese military police sitting on horses with bayonets pointing right at us! More than fifty of them!

They came at us—started beating up the crowd. Everybody panicked. Some marchers jumped right over the railing to the tracks below. Others were speared by the bayonets. Those soldiers on horseback rounded up people, tied them with ropes, and then went after more. They beat them with the handle end of the horse whip. I tried to hide but I guess since I was only ten, they left me alone.

YI SANGDO, (m) b. 1910, truck driver, Kyŏnggi Province:
My family said, "Today is the day to shout *mansei*." I went to the market in Osan city, full of people, coming from everywhere. People wore white clothes in those days, so on market day it was white everywhere. Not a single person wore colors.

I pushed my way into the crowd, and heard whispers that someone had a Korean flag. That was the first time in my life I ever saw a Korean flag. It was so interesting, so pretty, to my childish mind.

In Osan, Japanese merchants had many stores, and as we passed these stores, they were all shut tight.

Young men danced in the street, singing "Independence, independence." I followed them, fascinated. They carried torches as they moved along the streets.

The busy street of Honmachi, now Ch'ungmu-ro, Seoul,
with all signs in Japanese, circa 1920. (Norman Thorpe Collection)

The demonstrators headed toward the railroad station, but we ran into the Japanese army with rifles ready. Oh, I thought, so that is what the Japanese army looks like. The soldiers grabbed the Korean flag and struck at people with their bayonets. People fell like leaves. When one person fell, somebody else took up the cry, then got crushed, then another would take it up. All the time, the soldiers just beat them to a pulp.

When it got dark, I heard gunshots. It turned out they were blanks, to scare the people and make them go home. The police were tired by then. They began arresting people and taking them to the police station. My brother-in-law was arrested.

Later, the Police Commander released the prisoners, saying, "Go home, go home. Don't make trouble." Especially to the older men, he said, "Grandpa, why are you making trouble? Go home." He spoke kindly to these people. He unfastened the ropes that bound them and sent them home. It was the policemen who were kind. I don't know about other places, but that's what happened in our town.

The next day, Japanese soldiers went around searching for demonstrators, but they didn't bother those day-workers with *chige* (A-frame backpacks) on their backs. So that day, many who had never worked before put chiges on their backs. Soldiers called out, in clumsy Korean, "You there, where going?" When the men said, "Going to the field to pull weeds," the soldiers let them go. It was all right if they were out in the fields working. The soldiers just didn't want them to gather in groups.

KIM YŎSŎNG, (m) b. 1910, photographer, South P'yŏngan Province:
People in our small village climbed up on a hill, and at the top of our lungs we yelled, "Independence for Korea!" Nobody pushed us to do it. It was a natural, spontaneous outburst. There were just a few of us. Then we went around shouting *mansei* all day. No army, no police came. Our village was too small for them to bother with.

YI OKHYŎN, (f) b. 1911, housewife, North P'yŏngan Province:
We had our own demonstration for independence, but it was later, not on the first of March. We lived in a rural area, you know, and news reached there in waves. By the time we got the news, it was much later in March.

At school, my homeroom teacher was a woman named Mrs. Chang. One of my classmates was a young boy who later became a surgeon, famous enough to perform surgery on Kim Il Sŏng [president of communist North Korea, 1948–1994]. Yes, it was a co-ed class.

We were only eight years old, so we all simply followed the teacher. She took us to the top of a hill, and we all shouted *mansei* at the top of our lungs, then we just came down. Not much else happened. I don't remember any police coming.

CH'U PONGYE, (f) b. 1913, housewife, North Kyŏngsang Province:
After the *mansei* movement, they took my father to jail and beat him severely. The police claimed that he had joined the demonstration and yelled *mansei*. They came all the way to our small village to find him and haul him away.

They did not bother my brother because he was attending a Japanese school. Actually, because my father sent his son to get a Japanese education, the police kept father only one day and then released him. You have to remember that in those days very few people sent their children to Japanese schools with Japanese teachers.

PAK CHUN'GI, (f) b. 1914, housewife, Kyǒnggi Province:
I remember March First. I was only six, but I remember vividly that along the back wall of our yard, we had a lot of persimmon trees. Because of how the branches grew, we often had fun climbing them. That day, everyone said, "Let's go demonstrate," but Grandmother said, "Why can't we shout *mansei* from our own house?"

So we all climbed on the persimmon trees and shouted over the wall at the top of our lungs, "*Mansei, mansei.*"

Even I climbed up, it was so easy, but I had mixed emotions. In order to shout *mansei*, you know, you have to raise both arms in the air. I was afraid I might fall, so I stood up very timidly.

While we were doing all that, we noticed that people came out from the other houses shouting and waving flags. I remember dogs barking and Japanese soldiers with their long swords, beating people down right and left.

Since we were the first to shout, Grandmother and I trembled with fear, for we thought the soldiers were coming to get us. We went into an inner room and hid ourselves. I cried, and Grandmother held me tightly.

Policemen came by, making great noises, stamping their feet, but they passed our house and did not come in. We were spared. They went after the young men. Those young men were beaten and speared, slashed with the sabers, and I've seen it—they cut off some men's legs. It was just a gory scene. I heard crying and screaming.

My uncle, Mother's brother, was taken to prison. My maternal grandfather also went to prison because of independence activities, and for some reason, he stayed in prison ten years.

KIM SANGSUN, (m) b. 1916, gold miner, Kyǒnggi Province:
I don't remember the actual Independence Day—I was much too young. But I do remember, even a few years after the demonstrations, that for no good reason the Japanese came and arrested community leaders, imprisoned them, released them, and in general just made their lives miserable.

They considered my father one of those leaders because they knew he had been one of the demonstrators. He didn't want to be put in jail, so he hid in the mountains and moved from place to place to avoid arrest. My family took food to him in the mountains in secret, but sometimes in the evenings he would come down out of the mountain and spend time with us.

PAK SŎNGP'IL,
(m) b. 1917, farmer/fisherman, South Kyŏngsan Province:
I want to tell you about my aunt, Pak Sunch'ŏn. As a young woman, she taught at a girls' high school in Masan, a seaport west of Pusan. In 1919 she had a visit from Mr. Yi Kapsŏng, one of the thirty-three signers of the Declaration of Independence. Mr. Yi brought with him, in secret of course, the text of the declaration and a Korean flag. He gave these to my aunt and asked her to lead a demonstration in Masan on the same day as the one in Seoul. She printed copies of the declaration, then went out and led a demonstration.

Immediately she got arrested and thrown in prison, along with many of her students. But she was lucky. One of her students had parents who knew the Masan prison warden and they managed to have the warden close his eyes for a minute. My aunt disappeared.

That student's grandfather arranged a hiding place for my aunt in a remote village in Sunch'ŏn, Chŏlla Province. He said, "We'll say that you came here, to this remote place, to get married." It was a poor village, so she put on patched clothing. She stayed there in hiding for about a month. Her name was Pak Myŏngyŏl, but she changed it to Sunch'ŏn, meaning "obeying heaven," to hide her true identity.

Well, she couldn't live there for long, so her brother (my father) made plans to smuggle her into Japan. He hoped that the saying would be true, "It is darkest under the light."

She escaped to Tokyo. She actually went there for two reasons: first to hide, and second, to get higher education. She enrolled in college under her new name, but it didn't work. It took the Japanese police only six months to catch up with her and arrest her again. They sent her back to Masan prison and she served time there for one and a half years.

My aunt left many, many books at my home, packed in boxes and on shelves all over the house. The detectives took them, one or two at a time, so that all the shelves and boxes became empty. They just came and took them. Of course, we didn't dare try to stop them.

Change by Choice

My grandfather owned our property and it was quite large, but when my aunt was arrested and put in jail, her trial cost us a lot of money. Grandfather sold off much of the land to come up with the cash, so our holdings shrank greatly.

My whole family came under suspicion and police detectives came every single day to watch us. I must have been about seven or eight at the time, because I remember I had started primary school. The detectives asked us, whenever we returned home, where we'd been, what we'd done. They were constantly there.

After my aunt got out of prison, she returned to Tokyo and attended college there. She met a fellow Korean student named Pyŏn Hiyŏng who later became president of a university in Seoul. Mr. Pyŏn's family was prominent. His relatives included Pyŏn Yŏngt'ae, a foreign minister under Syngman Rhee. The Pyŏns often came to visit our house. Pyŏn Hiyŏng and my aunt married. It wasn't arranged; it was a love match.

YI CHAE'IM, (f) b. 1919, housewife, Kyŏnggi Province:
We knew about the martyr Yu Kwansun, a schoolgirl in Seoul. She was only sixteen when she led a March 3 demonstration. They arrested her, put her in prison, and there she was tortured and died. Such a young girl! Her story caught the imagination of everyone; it became a rallying cry.

Before I left for America, I went to see her statue. It was a winter day, and she was covered with snow. She had studied so hard, and now she was just standing there in the snow. I felt so bad. What had she done to deserve such a fate? The tears just ran down my face.

3 : A Map Changed My Life

HONG ŬLSU [HONG EUL SOO]

Teacher Turned Businessman (m) b. 1905, *South Kyŏngsang Province*

My father had no job when I was born. He was a Confucian scholar, a "superior man" (*sŏnbi*), so it was beneath his dignity to engage in any menial wage-earning work. In fact, you might define *sŏnbi* as a person who doesn't work. When it rains and the roof leaks, he sits there in his room with the rain pouring on his head. My father never applied for the civil service exam (*kwagŏ*) under the Chosŏn dynasty. He was a *sŏnbi* going nowhere.

I spent the first sixteen years of my life in the small village of Waesŏk, north of Yangsan city, South Kyŏngsang Province. My grandfather had built up quite a large farm, but my father gambled away the entire inheritance and our family barely survived.

DIRT POOR

For those who barely make a living there is a phrase, "*ch'ogŭn mokp'i,*" meaning grass roots and tree bark, and this is literally what we lived on. In the spring, we chopped off the previous year's growth of the pine branch and peeled off the surface layer. Inside is a sweet, oozing sap. We cut this off, drank some and dried the rest. Later we could soak it in water and rehydrate it. It has a very inviting aroma. It is called *mokp'i*, tree bark.

We also picked up acorns from the mountain in the autumn and ate them during the winter. These we had to soak for many days to get rid of the acrid smell and the caustic chemicals.

Yes, we really did live like that. Of all the households in the village, by February, only about five or six were still eating grains of any kind. We were all that poor, and our family was one of the poorest.

A typical Korean farm village of the early twentieth century.
(Norman Thorpe Collection)

Our village was in such a remote mountain area that tigers roamed freely, and behind our houses we had a tiger trap. We built collapsible stone walls with a wooden column in the middle. To the column, we tied a puppy. When a tiger came to attack the puppy, the shaking pulled loose the stones and they fell on top of the tiger.

I attended the village school (*sŏdang*) until I was fifteen. Then, in 1920, I was whisked off against my will to the Japanese primary school. Here's the story.

In those days, the Korean *sŏnbi* attitude was to forbid children going to those primary schools. They said children would turn into Japanese if they went to Japanese-built schools. So you see, my grandfather and my father, both being *yangban* (upper class) and *sŏnbi*, refused to let me go to school. Besides, the Japanese required each student to cut off his long hair if he attended that school.

So, now the school is open, but the children from *yangban* families are not attending. Obviously, this was not acceptable to the Japanese officials, so one day the county executive, the county police chief (a Japanese), the township chief, and the police branch chief all descended upon our *sŏdang* and demanded that it be closed.

They dragged all of us—literally by our long braids—to the township office courtyard. They had the hair clippers ready and proceeded to cut our hair. Right there. All of us had long hair, hanging down our backs in long braids. Then we were all sent home with no hair.

Grandfather took one look at me and went into a great rage. He yelled, "You became Japanese. Do not step inside this gate." So for three days I had to stay elsewhere. I begged Grandfather for forgiveness and he finally relented.

Because of my advanced age (I was already sixteen) and knowledge of Chinese characters, I began school as a second grader. The whole idea of primary school was so new that we felt no disgrace at beginning at such an age.

Those ten years old or younger, or those who did not know Chinese characters, entered first grade. Those who knew Chinese characters and Chinese literature began in second grade and studied only algebra and Japanese language. Third grade was for those who had finished second grade.

We had a Japanese principal and one Korean teacher—that was the entire staff. I do not believe the principal looked down on us Koreans as inferior. He was an educator, very interested in educating Koreans.

This principal had an interesting teaching method. He emphasized memorization. He taught something one day and then the next day he asked for the hands of students who had memorized the previous day's lesson. If you did this, once you got that day's lesson, you could go home. The third day, he asked for the hands of those who had memorized the previous two days, and so on. At the end of the semester, he asked for the hands of those who had memorized all four books of language and two books of arithmetic. I must tell you, I was the only one who could recite all of those six books.

A MAP CHANGED MY LIFE

The principal had a son who finished university in Japan and came to visit his father in our village. This young man was very good to the students and eager to befriend us. I remember him fondly. He kept encouraging us to study, learn, get an education. I think he felt sorry for us, we were so ignorant in this small, remote village tucked away in a southern corner of Korea.

"That's the only way you will improve your lot in life," he kept telling us. "Improve your own society, so you will come up to the level of us Japanese."

When school stopped for vacation in July of 1921, this young man told some of us, "When you have a break from farming, come and spend time with me."

Several of us did visit him. He showed us a map of the world. I had never seen a map before, and I had no idea what it was. It had such funny shapes and colors. He hung it on the wall and asked, "Do you know where Korea is on this map?"

Of course we could not answer him. Remember, I was sixteen and I had not even gone to Yangsan city, which is only eight miles away. So we were all stumped by his question. I knew of a country called China, and I knew of Russia and Japan. I thought that comprised the entire world. I had not even heard of other countries.

He pointed to a spot on the map and said, "This is Korea, and here is Japan. You are surrounded by Russia, China, and Japan. There are other countries farther away, like France, Germany, and America."

I was stunned. I was so struck by my own ignorance, I thought, How ignorant can I be? It is one thing to be a frog in a small well, but this is ridiculous. When I saw that Japan was only a little larger than Korea, it gave me confidence that if Japan could do things, then we could do them, too.

I resolved to broaden my knowledge and get an education. All thanks to that young teacher, I could no longer be content with knowing just the Chinese characters. I had to know the world.

To do that, I determined to go to Japan.

Now remember, my father and grandfather hated the Japanese, so I knew they would never give me permission to travel. Because of the new relaxed rule that began in 1920, travelers between Japan and Korea no longer needed passports, but I still did need a residence registration. I knew that Father, who now worked as town clerk, would never issue the papers, so I got them from another clerk on a day when father stayed home ill.

GOING TO JAPAN

Next I needed travel money. I knew my mother had secretly accumulated a tiny bit of money, seven yen and ninety sen, that she was saving for my marriage. [In 1920, one month living in a boarding house cost 15 yen.]

I must tell you how Mother earned that money. She left home at dawn every morning and went into the mountains where charcoal was being prepared in a cave. She carried two charcoal bundles down from the mountain to Yangsan town to sell. She couldn't carry two bundles on her head, so she carried one bundle half way, put it down and left it, went back and got the other one. In this relay fashion, she took both bundles into Yangsan. Thirty li round trip, so it was always late at night when she got home.

Let me tell you how brave Mother was. Because she was often out late at night, she encountered tigers three different times. Tigers, she said, when they attack human beings, paw the ground, dig up gravel and throw it at humans. Then they growl menacingly. If, when the tiger is doing this, you get frightened and start running away, it will attack and devour you. If you don't lose your composure and just walk on, however, ignoring him, the tiger will lose interest and slink away. Easier said than done—but Mother did it, three times, so she must have been a really strong person.

Now back to the money. I wanted to use it to go to Japan, so the next morning when Mother was in the kitchen working, I secretly took the money and told Mother I was going to school. I felt so guilty that I could not eat a bit of breakfast. Mother thought I was sick.

I left home and walked eighteen miles to the town of Mulgŭm to catch the train to Pusan. I bought a ticket that included the train to Pusan, the ferry between Pusan and Japan, and a train in Japan from Shimonoseki to Osaka. It cost seven yen, so now in my pocket there were only ninety sen left.

Until then, I had never laid eyes on a train. What an impressive sight! A huge, black monster. I was fascinated by how it was able to move all by itself. I took that train and arrived at the Pusan station near the harbor, and took the ship to Japan.

When I got to Japan, I boarded the lowest-class train, a freight train with only one passenger car, and arrived at the Osaka station in the middle of the night. The whole city was full of lights. Shining. Blinking. For a country hick like me, it was fascinating. Especially the neon lights that flashed red, blue, and green. I thought it was a ghost playing tricks on me.

At the station I tried to get into the third-class restroom, but it was very crowded, so I went to the one next door. It was empty—and I, in my ignorance, had no idea it was a first-class restroom.

There it was, a western-style flush toilet. I had no idea how to use that contraption. I squatted on top of the seat and my feet kept slipping off. It

Change by Choice

was the most uncomfortable situation I had ever been in. I thought, This does not make sense. How can wealthy, civilized people use such uncomfortable equipment?

While I was struggling with this, all of a sudden the toilet flushed with a terrible rush of water! I thought I had broken something. My only thought was not to get arrested for breaking something in the restroom, so I could not even do my job, I just ran out as fast as I could. It turned out that the station periodically flushed the toilets and it just happened to be while I was struggling with it.

My clothes at the time were the Korean traditional clothes (*hanbok*). In those days, the poor farm people changed into a set of winter clothes at the end of September and wore them day and night until the following April. All during that time, they did not wash their clothes or take baths. You know that *hanbok* is white, so by spring it was almost black because of the accumulated dirt, and that is what I had on. It was January, so I had been in the same clothes for more than three months.

On my feet I wore straw sandals; I did not even know about leather shoes. So here I was, in the middle of Osaka, Japan, with dirty, smelly Korean clothes and straw sandals. No wonder people in the train would not sit next to me, with such a strong odor from my clothes.

A RURAL VILLAGE

From the station, I headed for the residence of a man from my village who lived in Osaka. I lived with this man and the man's son for three months and worked to save money to enter school. With the friend's help, we two boys got into a commercial middle school in a rural village away from Osaka city. We lived in an abandoned house, and the father, on the fifteenth of each month, sent us rice and other food.

People in the village—simple, generous folk—said to us, "You must feel very lonesome, having come so far away from your home town and being in a foreign country."

ON MY OWN IN TOKYO

Soon I moved to Tokyo, got a job delivering newspapers, and then moved on to selling a kind of snack food, a bean called *natto*. To make money to pay room and board, I had to sell fifteen packs of *natto*s each day. If I didn't sell enough, I just went without food.

Next I attended trade school, but soon gave that up and entered Ch'ungsik Middle School, a prep school oriented toward higher education.

In Japan in those days there were late-night markets, mostly run by the *yakuza*, the Japanese underground organization. I found a job as an apprentice, and this new boss was indeed a *yakuza*. He fed his workers three meals a day, and gave us ten yen a month. Most amazing, he paid the money needed for us to go to school. The first time I went to meet him, he gave me a dish full of rice. White rice. I devoured it. I said to myself, Now, I have arrived!

When I finished the apprenticeship selling books, my boss gave me a spot of my own in the market. Every month I had to pay him the whole amount that I made and out of that he gave me a salary.

I went to school during the day and worked at the market at night. By the time the market closed and we cleaned up, I got to my room after eleven o'clock at night. Finally then I could eat my supper. Next I studied until three in the morning. I slept only about three hours a day.

Soon younger boys were apprenticed to me, and I diligently taught them all I knew. For example, the way to sell books in the *yakuza* marketplace was to have a conspirator pretend to be a customer. He buys a book from you, and then makes a big noise about how great the book is, and how he can't wait to get home to read it. All the people who hear him believe him and innocently decide that they, too, need the same book.

While I worked in the late-night market, I also applied to a prestigious second-rank middle school, but they turned down my application because of the uncertainty of my income. Finally, in 1925, I settled on a third-rank middle school, and once in, I did all right, ranking either at the top or second in my class.

In that school we had four classes in each grade, labeled A, B, C, D. A Korean called Pak was in class A and I was in class B, and both of us were at the top in our respective classes. It made me very proud to have Koreans at the top of Japanese classes.

Pak also was putting himself through school, but he was always starving and behind in his payments. I lent him tuition money several times but finally had him come live with me so we could eat and work together. I figured I could work a few days more and make enough money for both of us. At first he was embarrassed, but he was so grateful he jumped up and down.

Once we moved in together, he became much more settled and happy, and could concentrate on his studies. When my *yakuza* boss found out, he scolded me for doing this without his permission, but after the scolding, he said I was really doing a good thing and he raised my salary.

Early in 1926 I knelt before my *yakuza* boss and waited for his instructions. He said he once had ambitions, just like me, to put himself through school by working in the night market, but he failed in his studies and got stuck in the business world. "I don't want you to end up the way I did," he said. "Before it is too late, you must leave this business."

"I will never forget the kindness you have shown me," I answered him, "so please don't make me leave."

He smiled and said, "No, you must study more and get a higher education. To make it easier for you, I will set up another marketplace for you." This was an unusual kindness of this *yakuza* boss.

Also, once, a while back, I had turned down a raise he offered, and now I found that, unknown to me, he saved all that extra money every month and gave it to me now as a bank account. I was so overcome, I bowed my head to the floor many, many times. I repeated to myself my favorite motto in life, "Where there is a will there is a way."

Because of his help, I was able to drop some of my workload, and instead of working every single night I cut back to working only half the month. My living finally became comfortable.

UNIVERSITY DECISIONS

I decided to become a teacher of English, so I chose to attend Aoyama Christian University because of its excellent reputation. It was operated by missionaries and many of the faculty were Americans. I wanted to learn English from native speakers. In 1932 I graduated from Aoyama, but there are some university experiences I'd like to share.

During the first year in college I joined a study group on campus, studying communism. Over thirty students attended this group, all Japanese except for me. We got along just fine. They would hold my hand and say, "We will all work together to drive the Japanese out of your country. We are in this together."

Most of the Korean students in Japan became infatuated with communism. The Russian revolution was only a few years back, and communism was the new force. It was well organized, systematic, logically reasoned out, or so I thought, and also the Communist Party in Japan had as one of its slogans, "Independence for Korea."

I'll tell you why. The main objective of the Japanese Communist Party was to overthrow the Japanese Imperial government. They reasoned that by helping Korea become independent, Japan would lose a tremendous source of income, the government would fall, and the Communists could step in. Therefore, it was in their own interest to recruit Korean students to join with them to overthrow the Imperial government.

The Communists required you to fight for their ideology, not just study and talk, so in my second year, I became the leader of the study group and a fervent activist for the Communist ideology. We met secretly once a month to publish and distribute pamphlets. We never told each other our names or our addresses; only our uniforms indicated what university we attended. This secrecy protected each of us in case police arrested and tortured us. We could honestly say we did not know who else was in the movement.

I also became active among the Korean students at various universities in Tokyo. In early February 1929, seventeen Korean students secretly met to plan the tenth anniversary of the 1919 Korean Independence Movement. As soon as the meeting began, the police swooped down upon us and hauled us off to jail. Obviously, we had a spy somewhere within our group.

I stayed in a Tokyo prison for twenty-nine days, beginning that day in February. Very cold. Every other day they took us to the interrogation room and asked what we did, what group we joined, whom we met, who were our contacts, and the names and addresses of any others. I answered consistently, "I don't know. There are none." Then they beat me severely.

While in our cells, they did not allow us to open our mouths. No talking all day. Just sit. If we disobeyed, they beat us again. So we sat.

I had plenty of time to think. Before going to jail, I had kept busy working in the night market, going to school, studying homework, attending the reading club, and printing pamphlets. But now, in jail with nothing to do but sit all day, I began to rethink my life.

If I continued along the present course, sometime in the future I would be arrested again and put in jail for a long time. I really did not mind if I died for my convictions, but I would be shirking my responsibilities to my parents and causing my family much trouble. There is a traditional Confucian saying, "Govern yourself, manage the family, and then govern the country." I said to myself, I must first govern myself and then help out my family and my country. I thought of many questions about communism and there seemed to be no answers that satisfied me. I decided to abandon communism. I declared to my comrades that I would no longer participate in their activities. They called me a quitter.

I was released from prison without being indicted. From then on, I concentrated on my studies and improved my grades. I graduated from Aoyama University in 1932, with a teaching credential.

In order to learn English correctly, I decided I should go to America. The faculty members, having seen a great change in me from a bothersome rabble-rouser to such a studious young man, and also knowing that I was putting myself through college, took a liking to me and said they would help me get to America.

Well, it never happened. Relations between Japan and the United States deteriorated badly, so I stayed at Aoyama and earned another degree, in theology, in 1935.

The world situation kept getting worse, so I decided to return to Korea. The American Southern Methodists helped me get a teaching position in one of their schools in Korea. They warned me to be careful—Japanese in Korea were not nearly as friendly as those in Japan itself.

I BECOME A TEACHER

I was full of emotion when stepping back on Korean soil after fourteen years in Japan. I started teaching English at the Holston Girls' High School in Kaesŏng, Kyŏnggi Province, in April 1935.

In those days, the Confucian custom of separating males and females still prevailed in many situations, and thus before I started this teaching job, they told me to be very careful as a male teacher in a classroom full of adolescent girls. They said, treat everyone equally, do not look too long in one direction so as not to arouse suspicion that you are favoring some pretty girl.

After one year, Paehwa Middle School in Seoul [founded by U.S. Methodists in 1898] asked me to join its faculty, and in the end I went down to Seoul. I was told that I would learn a lot from Mr. Yi, the vice principal at Paehwa. He was a nationalist and also a wise man. No one said outright that he was a nationalist, of course, because in those days if you said it outright, everybody would get into trouble. Mr. Yi wanted me at Paehwa because he refused to speak Japanese. Since I spoke fluent Japanese, I could be his interpreter whenever he had to meet with the government officials. I would thus be taking care of administrative details for him, and also learning how to deal with the Japanese in Korea.

Even this job did not work out for me. The police detectives' continual harassment put an end to my teaching career by the end of this second year. The High Police arrived at least once a month to check on me as part of their surveillance of politically suspect activists. This harassment gradually became more intense, until finally the police specifically told me to resign from teaching—otherwise, to get me out, they might close down the entire school. Reluctantly, I resigned and moved to Pusan.

A BUSINESSMAN

In April of 1937 I went back into business. I set up shop in Pusan and began shipping huge containers of cotton to Osaka, Japan. I was in this business until the beginning of the Second World War.

Life was good. We lived comfortably, and during that time, with the money I made, I resumed my role as eldest son. I bought a house, rice paddies and fields for my brother to expand our family's holdings so my parents and grandfather could live comfortably, and I helped my younger siblings whenever they had need. That was the least I could do to make up for taking off to Japan so many years ago with Mother's hard-earned money.

In the early 1940s, the colonial government put more and more restrictions on Koreans. If three adults wanted to get together, they had to have a permit to assemble, or else they would get hauled into jail for anti-Japanese activities. About this time, I met a newspaper reporter, and we struck up an immediate friendship. We shared frustrations over the suffering inflicted by the Japanese and, in spite of the restrictions, decided to form a secret society.

Outwardly we made it sound harmless, so we could get together without arousing suspicion. We named the society the "Thirty-sixers" because we were both that age, and we limited it to twelve members who were both our same age and had at least a high school education. As a goal, we planned to educate and sensitize others about the oppressive Japanese rule. We decided to be responsible for enlightening five people each. After a year, seven of the ten we had mentored joined our group.

To meet like this was extremely dangerous and required great secrecy and preparation. At each meeting we shared information about the domestic and war situations, the forced draft, unfair taxation, and changing names from Korean to Japanese. Then we tried to find ways to publicize all this information.

As a businessman, I knew the advantage of cultivating friendship with people in high positions, so when I built my factory in Pusan, I befriended a policeman. This man eventually got promoted to the Japanese High Police staff as a detective with the job of watching the independence activists and radical agitators. The policeman and I got together at least once a month and I plied him with liquor and sometimes gave him money.

Once when we were eating and drinking together my friend said, laughing all the time, "You know, the secret police have a blacklist of educated Koreans and anti-Japanese activists. When the order comes, the police will round up and execute those on the list. You are on the list."

He recommended that I move to a small farm or village where nobody knew me, and sit out the duration of the war. I heeded his advice. I closed the business and bought an apple orchard in Kyŏngsan, just south of Taegu, in North Kyŏngsang Province, and moved my family there. In that county, only two Koreans had orchards as large as mine. Japanese owned all the others.

I now acted like a gentleman farmer. I told my hired workers only that I had been a businessman in Pusan and when the war came I decided to move to a rural area and become a farmer. I said nothing more about my past—prison, teaching, detectives—to anyone.

It turned out that orchard work was interesting—spraying, pruning, picking. To keep busy, I put on dirty clothes, dirty shoes, and worked right alongside my workers.

Even though we lived in the country, I read the *Asahi Shinbun*, a huge Tokyo newspaper, and I had a very good-quality radio. Through these I concluded that Japan would lose the war.

On the *Asahi* staff there was a special correspondent named Moriguchi, stationed in Berlin. He wrote articles detailing the world situation and hinted that Japan was at a great disadvantage. He never came out and said anything specific, for his writing had to pass the censorship board. But between the lines I read of Japan's eventual doom. Ordinary people might not see it, but others could draw that conclusion.

Remember my police friend in Pusan had told me about a blacklist of people who would be rounded up at the end, and killed? He was joking, I thought. But near the end of the war, that Moriguchi columnist in Berlin vanished. Just disappeared. I think he himself was on this hate list. Even a Japanese, stationed far away in Berlin for a great newspaper, was eliminated. So the list must have been real.

When I heard the news that General Tojo had resigned, I invited the "Thirty-sixers" to my orchard. We concluded that Japan was indeed losing the war to America, and we decided to form a committee to help govern Korea after the war was over. We patted ourselves on our backs for planning so far ahead.

LIBERATION

One day, I heard on my radio that the following day there would be an important announcement. I dare say, it seemed that nobody else in the Kyŏngsan area knew about it. I ran into the county chief, a Korean, and told him I was sure that the Japanese would surrender. He was dubious. "Is that so?" he asked.

I went home and listened to my radio. The Japanese Emperor came on the radio and surrendered. The war was over. We were free. *Free.* August 15, 1945.

EPILOGUE, 1945–1995

Upon hearing the news, Mr. Hong went directly to Pusan and joined with others to form a self-governing committee in hopes that when the Americans arrived, this committee would be allowed to run the province. The United States army ignored them. However, because Mr. Hong spoke English better than anyone else, the Americans asked him to work with them as interpreter and gave him "some fancy title."

The U.S. Army said Mr. Hong could take over one of the empty factory buildings left behind by the Japanese, so he restarted his cotton textile business in Pusan. He "made lots of money, then lost lots of money."

Mr. Hong joined the Rotary Club, and in 1961 he also helped found the Korean Lions Club International.

In 1970 the Korean government appointed him to a ten-person team representing business, trade, insurance, construction, and manufacturing that was sent to visit ten countries in Europe to see how Europeans conducted business. The team then made recommendations to the Korean government on how to improve the Korean business climate.

Mr. Hong left the group at the end of its tour, and went on his own to visit India, Southeast Asia, Hong Kong, and America. At retirement, he joined his children in America. He is a past president of the San Francisco Korean Senior Citizen's Association.

4 : Choosing an Education

Every family must decide if, and how, to educate its children. In Korea before the 1890s, that choice was simple, for the only school available was the male bastion *sŏdang*, village school. Here, the local boys studied Chinese writing and Confucian precepts under the guidance of a male teacher. Then, around the turn of the century, many western-style schools began to be built, and by 1910 Koreans could choose among modern schools built by Koreans, by newly arrived missionaries, or by the Japanese.

The most common school for boys continued to be the ancient *sŏdang*, which posed no threat to the new rulers, for in them students learned only time-honored Chinese classics and Confucian ideals of hierarchy and loyalty. Two of the men gave their memories of this type of school.

HONG ŬLSU [HONG EUL SOO],
(m) b. 1905, teacher, South Kyŏngsang Province:
We were so poor that we had a hard time paying our *sŏdang* master. Students took turns taking food to his house. Other than that, he got paid only once a year, after the harvest, when the parents presented him with part of the crop, mostly rice, in proportion to the family's wealth.

The Chinese text that we learned was designed by the Chinese to familiarize students with the culture of China. These texts were nothing but Chinese history, poetry, stories about warriors and artists, you name it. So, insidiously, they fostered respect for the strong foreign country and its culture [the syndrome called *sadae*], making us think that if it is foreign, from a strong country, it must be good.

In the beginning I finished my Thousand Characters (*Ch'ŏn Ja Mun*),

Traditional Confucian school for boys (sŏdang), *circa 1900–1905. (Norman Thorpe Collection)*

then I studied Chinese history in twelve volumes (*Tong Myŏng Sŏn Sŭp, Myŏng Sim Bo Gam,* and *Tong Gam*). Next came the seven volumes of Mencius and another volume of *T'ae Hak,* then seven volumes of *Non Ŏ,* called Four Writings (*Sa Sŏ*) and Three Chronicles (*Sam Gyŏng*). When you finish these, you are accorded the status of a semi-Confucian scholar. Even in the local *sŏdang,* you acquire this status. Then you go on to composing Chinese poetry in Chinese characters.

YI SANGDO, (m) b. 1910, truck driver, Kyŏnggi Province:

All of us were at different levels of learning, all in the same room, over twenty children. Teacher sat there on the mat against one wall, smoking his long pipe. All twenty of us sat around him. He got us started and then he just watched everybody. We read and read and read and tried to memorize, all day long.

Our teacher was very strict. He made us concentrate on our studies. If we even looked sideways, he whopped our heads with his switch. Always the head. It hurt. After a while he would say, "Let's take a break." Then we could have lunch, and after lunch, resume. When it was supper time, we could go home.

Fourteen of the men interviewed had begun their education in their local sŏdang, but at some point ten of those transferred to the new western-style schools. Two of the oldest men spoke for those who stayed away from the new schools because of tradition, poverty, or anti-Japanese sentiment. Pak Tuyang (b. 1900): "Father was a farmer. He said if you attend Japanese school, they will cut off your long braid, so he would not permit me to attend," and Kim Saenggwang (b. 1912) echoed: "There was a Japanese primary school nearby, but my father refused to let us attend, saying, if we went there, they would eat us alive."

KIM HOJUN, (m) b. 1918, farmer, Hwanghae Province:
My family was progressive. I am one of five sons and we have three sisters, and my parents put all eight of us through school. Our neighbors in the village wagged their fingers at us. "What good is it to learn at the hand of the Japanese?" they asked. Remember, this was just a small farm village. Perhaps it was my own attitude, but I never felt any animosity toward the Japanese. It just didn't occur to me that they were persecuting us.

CHŎNG KŬMJAE, (m) b. 1919, day laborer, North Ch'ungch'ŏng Province:
I lived in a poor farm village; however, right across the river from our village is Kyŏnggi Province and there, in the larger town, was a French Catholic parochial school. I attended that school. The principal was a French priest, and we called him Priest Im. All the teachers were Korean.
We learned in Korean until the third grade. Then the edict came down to do all teaching in Japanese. Since the teachers themselves did not speak Japanese very well, we really struggled together. In order to make us speak in Japanese, no matter how poorly, they gave each of us ten tickets. If, during class, somebody spoke in Korean, then they took away one ticket. If all ten got taken away, they lowered your grade.

YI SANGDO, (m) b. 1910, truck driver, Kyŏnggi Province:
In those days there were still many boys with long hair in braids, and one of the rules of the new Japanese primary schools was to cut off the long

hair. Since I grew up in the city, I didn't have long hair to begin with. Those other boys, the ones from the country, had to cut their hair.

In my class some older boys talked down to me [used a lower level of speech]. So we eleven-year-olds stuck together and said, "Hey, we are all in the first grade and we are all learning the first sounds of the Japanese alphabet. You are no better than us. We are equal." I noticed that these older ones learned a lot slower than we did—apparently they had too many distracting thoughts. They were taller, but duller.

The town had another primary school for the Japanese children. We never had any trouble with those kids. It's not that we got along well, they just avoided us. Their parents told them not to play with Korean kids. You know how Korean boys are, when they fight, they just go all out and get wild! Japanese boys didn't fight like that.

KANG SANG'UK [KANG SANG WOOK],
(m) b. 1935, physicist, North P'yŏngan Province:
Every summer vacation our school teachers told us to keep a diary and do one project. Every summer. I hated it. I'd wait until a week before school started and then make up a story to turn in as a diary. One year, about third or fourth grade, I did my project on the dragonflies that filled our valley. Books always showed kids using nets to catch insects. I tried to make a net but it didn't work, so I caught them by hand, pinching them right behind their wings. I tacked the dragonflies onto a board with pins and let them dehydrate. I ended up with twenty-five different shapes, sizes, and colors. I was proud to get so many.

For many of my school projects, I used Father's leather-bound *Encyclopedia Japonica*. He owned all thirty-seven volumes and all in Japanese. It rivaled the *Encyclopaedia Britannica*. When I was small I loved to "read" it—actually, look at the pictures. I was fascinated. Before the Second World War the printing was very good and the colored pictures were excellent. I especially loved pictures of lakes. Not ponds, not oceans. Lakes. I had never seen a lake. I would ask, "Why don't we have lakes in Korea?"

In school, our classes had sixty kids to a room with the teacher up front, and one speed of teaching for everybody. Discipline wasn't a problem, because students had to respect the teacher, and also the teacher could punish any bad behavior.

For punishment, teachers used switches made from acacia branches because they were the most supple branches and really hurt. They'd whip our calves, not vital organs, but, oh, it hurt. Some teachers slapped students on the cheek. Once the kid ducked and teacher hit his ear instead. He lost his hearing but his parents just accepted it.

Another favorite punishment combined pain with humiliation. The offender had to stand in front of class and with arms held straight out, hold heavy books or a pail of water at arm's length. That is torture. I know, because in second grade the teacher thought I was being disruptive by talking to the kids in the next seat, so he punished me that way.

I am told I was always full of mischief and never still. My own opinion is that I was full of energy and life.

In 1929, in the town of Kwangju, three Japanese male high school students insulted three Korean girl high school students waiting for a train. A clash ensued between Korean and Japanese students and quickly escalated into open fighting. The conflict spread all across Korea, and in the end hundreds of students were expelled from school and over a thousand were arrested. The repercussions lasted for years and reached, as one story shows, all the way down to first and second grades.

CHŎNG CHAESU, (m) b. 1923, shipyard draftee, North Chŏlla Province: One morning when I was in second grade [1931], they told all of us to assemble on the school grounds, and Japanese detectives surrounded us. They all rode horseback; I was terrified!

Nearby, the high school students had rioted, so to prevent us primary kids from getting involved, the mounted police came every day for almost a year. They could do this because there was only one Korean primary school in our town, which made it easy for the police to come and watch us.

Girls, on the other hand, never had attended any school. Daughters remained under the rule of their fathers and then their husbands, and now parents were encouraged to release these daughters, at least in part, into the care of unknown teachers. Some women interviewed had never attended school, and their attitudes, even now, ranged from docile to demanding. Kim Sŏbun, speaking of her own grandmother, also reminds us that intelligence does not depend on literacy.

KIM SŎBUN, (f) b. 1914, housewife, South Kyŏngsang Province:

My grandmother was quite a person. When Grandfather died, she ran the farm by herself. She never learned to read or write, but in her grain storehouse she kept a brush and India inkwell. With those she made long lines and short lines, for people she hired to work on the farm. She said the lines were the wages the workers should be paid. She had her own code system and she made no mistakes.

She ruled with an iron hand, including my father. He did not dare talk back to her. Once there was a dispute about water rights on the island. When grandmother showed up, they all calmed down and listened to her—and they were all men and she a woman.

YI OKPUN, (f) b. 1914, housewife, South Ch'ungch'ŏng Province:

Did I go to a *sŏdang*? What? Those places? Girls didn't go there! Girls should learn how to sew and cook. Learning that other kind of thing is not important.

My elder brothers all went to primary school. They insisted that I also go, but our mother was dead set against it. "Girls don't need to learn such things," she said. "It will all be wasted."

In spite of her objections, I did go to school for a little while—a month, maybe—when I was a teenager. I tried to study *han'gŭl* (Korean script). My brothers thought I should go, but nobody else did, so I quit.

My grandmother, my mother's mother, said to me, "It's better if you get married and start a new household—the sooner the better." So she married me off when I was only sixteen and my groom was eighteen.

PAK CHUN'GI, (f) b. 1914, housewife, Kyŏnggi Province:

Father considered himself to be a Confucian scholar and he wouldn't do any work, so we lived in poverty. Mother, however, was of a modern bent. She had gone to Seoul to Ewha Mission Girls' School, and she was in the second class to graduate. After she got married, she bore seven children and taught all of us at home, a modern education, just like at school.

I am still disappointed that I never got a real education. I couldn't understand or keep up with what folks said or what was happening outside the house, especially in the Japanese language. If I had known Japanese, I could have found out what they were thinking and what made them tick.

Then maybe I could have acted with more certainty. As it was, I had no confidence.

When I was eighteen, I got married. In those days, we didn't worry about getting along well, we just got along. I was always afraid of my husband. We didn't fight, because I wouldn't dare challenge him. He had a strong personality. He was such an honest, straight-arrow person that everyone trusted him, but if something went wrong outside, then he came home and took it out on me. I always said, "I'm sorry, I'm sorry," without even knowing what it was about. Since I always obeyed, to outsiders it looked like we were a harmonious couple, but inside, I often was not happy.

My husband had a transportation business, carrying supplies from one place to another. When the Second World War started, and things were rationed, even some Japanese families didn't have enough to eat, and they came to our house asking for handouts of the things that he transported.

YI CHAE'IM, (f) b. 1919, housewife, Kyŏnggi Province:
Our household was so traditional that when Grandfather came home from an outing, we all had to go out to the front gate and bow low; we were that strict. In *yangban* (upper class) tradition, Grandfather separated girls and boys at age seven. As a girl, I was confined to the inner rooms and never got out at all until I got married. Grandfather taught me Chinese characters, even though I was a girl, because he was a scholar in Chinese literature.

YU TŎKHŬI, (f) b. 1931, housewife, Kangwŏn Province:
I was ten [1941] and never had gone to school. Where I lived with my father at the gold mines, there wasn't any school, and Father said it was too far to go to the village. So I had never been to school at all. I don't know if it was because I was a girl or really there was no school nearby.

When I became ten, I insisted that I wanted to go to school. I threw a tantrum! I stamped my feet and cried my eyes out. Finally they separated me from my family so I could go to school. I stayed with relatives.

In order to enroll me, my father invited the Japanese principal to the only restaurant in town, and entertained him with a sumptuous dinner. Of course, I wasn't allowed into the restaurant, so I waited in the courtyard, and the next morning I started school. I guess feeding the principal did the trick.

Children whose families sent them to the new Japanese-built schools showed their willingness to trade various levels of oppression for the gift of new knowledge. On the other hand, several Japanese teachers, especially in primary school, went out of their way to befriend Korean students. In addition, two women interviewed had the unusual experience of attending schools reserved for Japanese children.

KIM SŎBUN, (f) b. 1914, housewife, South Kyŏngsang Province:
A young Japanese man, just graduated from Chinju Normal School, came to Sach'ŏn as our teacher. He influenced us greatly.

Three of us girls were in the class, the rest were all boys. After class this Japanese teacher gathered us three girls together and asked about Korean words. He would say Japanese words and ask for their Korean counterparts. We thought, among ourselves, that he did this so he would get a higher salary by being more fluent in Korean.

We planned to go on to girls' high schools, and to get ready for the entrance exam we attended extra classes after school. We girls took these classes along with the boys, but the boys always gave us a hard time. Yes, indeed, they really bullied us. After a while the Japanese teacher decided to teach us girls separately. One night he came to my house and the next night to another girl's house, back and forth. He did this for three months. He really put himself out for us.

Even after we moved on to high school, he rode on his bicycle from Sach'ŏn to Masan and Chinju, alternately, encouraging first the two girls in Masan and then me in Chinju.

Much later, when he was sixty-five and I was sixty, this teacher came from his home in Japan to visit Sach'ŏn, his home in Korea. After forty years. We were delighted to have this reunion with him.

PAK C. [ANONYMOUS], (f) b. 1927, housewife:
For one year, sixth grade, I moved down to Seoul and attended a special school where all the other students were Japanese and children of the nobility and high government officials. It was just like the *Gakushu-in* school [a school for the children of Japanese nobility in Japan itself]. The teachers used respectful language even to us little kids.

I don't remember that the Japanese teachers made me conscious of being Korean and thus different from themselves. I think I was brain-

Change by Choice

washed to identify with them. Oh, this mind game is truly terrifying, it is so effective. I knew so little about my own country.

I read many Japanese novels as a teenager, written by people like Kikuchi Kan. In school we read those novels even during class, sneaking them under the desk, circulating them among classmates, especially love stories. After all, we were adolescent girls.

KIM P. [ANONYMOUS], (f) b. 1931, housewife:
My father worked as carpenter for the Japanese hospital in Seoul, and we lived on the hospital grounds. I went to a Japanese elementary school with the Japanese kids. Only Japanese students went there, except for me. This was unusual. I believe it's because the Japanese people with whom my father worked really liked him. That's why they said to send me to the same school their kids attended.

Our school lunch was always packed with rice and a slice of brown pickle called *gobo*, and it never varied. I got sick of it. I just couldn't eat it.

I had close friendships with my Japanese classmates, but now, after so many years, I don't remember any names.

The few Koreans who continued on to high school became increasingly conscious of the different treatment they received. Many of them, especially those in Christian schools, found subtle ways to express anti-Japanese feelings.[1] However, the colonial government gradually closed down many of the indigenous schools, calling them "strongholds of actual or potential anti-Japanese sentiment."[2]

YANG SŎNGDŎK,
(m) b. 1919, electrical engineer, South Ch'ungch'ŏng Province:
In our town there was no separate Japanese elementary school, so the Japanese teacher's children attended our Korean primary school. We were children. We got along. I do not recall any conflicts among groups in the classroom along national lines.

In high school, things changed. Now, two-thirds of the class were Japanese. For the first time I experienced cliques forming along national lines, in class, after class, and outside the school grounds. We formed our own group, and the Japanese students formed their own groups.

It was impossible to have friends among the Japanese students. If I did that, I would be branded pro-Japanese and persecuted by my classmates. It was the same for the Japanese kids. If we ran into each other outside of school, on the street, the first thought we had was alertness, wariness, or hostility, not welcome or friendship.

KIM T. [ANONYMOUS], (m) b. 1919, factory worker:

I attended Sungin Commercial High School in P'yŏngyang, a Christian school created by Mr. Cho Mansik,[3] a well-known anti-Japanese activist. While there I became aware of discrimination. At this school, they heightened our awareness of and pride in being Korean and fostered a sense of active resistance against the Japanese.

Mr. Cho himself came once a week and gave us an inspirational talk. He could not come out and say that the Japanese were our unwelcome masters and we should resist, but in the form of a sermon from the Bible, he said those things. We did not mistake his message.

To show our anger at the Japanese, we found innocuous reasons to strike. We struck against the rule forbidding students to be married, or because we decided some teacher was no good.

The form of our strikes? We cut class. The word got around and nobody showed up. We would do it once, and one or two guys got disciplined. Then we'd wait a while and do it again, and one or two others would get in trouble. I was punished once. They whipped my calf with three bamboo strips tied into a long bar. They didn't just pretend to hit; they whipped with power and energy. I was black and blue for weeks.

Remember, this was a Christian school, founded by a Korean, so our teachers themselves had anti-Japanese sentiments, but they were careful not to let the news of our strikes get out—all our activities were confined to the campus. Once word leaked out that a certain school took part in anti-Japanese activities, the Japanese came to close down that school.

We had lots of strikes, but we had to make sure the reasons did not appear to be anti-Japanese. It wasn't very effective, I agree, but in those days, that was the most you could do, the watching and punishment were so severe.

I still remember a sad scene from my college days, when the president of our college, Dr. Underwood, son of the original missionary Dr. Underwood, left the campus with his rucksack on his back, trudging past our dormitory window. We watched him depart as a prisoner, going to some detention camp. We shed many, many tears for him, we felt so bad. That was a very bitter moment.

Change by Choice

U CH'AN'GU,

(m) b. 1916, railway worker, North Ch'ungch'ŏng Province:

My worst day came in January 1934, my third year in the agricultural high school. We came to school one snowy morning and saw a huge caravan of expensive cars coming to the school grounds. We were curious and thought some important person must be visiting.

Then the school office boy came to my classroom with a small piece of paper. When Teacher read the paper, his face went pale and his hand began to shake. He said to me, "You are summoned to the principal's office." The way he went so pale warned me that something bad was about to happen.

When I got to the office, seven other students already stood there, surrounded by detectives. The principal said, "You are summoned to the police station. You must go now."

The detectives started to handcuff us, but the principal spoke up and said, "Not here. This is just a school. Do it outside if you must." So they did.

The detectives put all of us in prison for twenty-nine days, with no summons, no nothing. On the thirtieth day, they took us out, put all our possessions in small bags, and took us to another police station for another twenty-nine days. They made that switch *five times*. It turned out that they had a rule that without any investigation or hearing, they could detain a person for only twenty-nine days. So they were trying to follow that law, going through the motion of releasing us, but as soon as we were out of the station, they took us again to another place for another twenty-nine days.

In the third prison, torture began. They had gotten wind of a plot to have a nationwide student uprising, and they thought we were part of it. They feared it might be a repeat of the Kwangju student uprising that swept the country. They wanted to nip it in the bud.

I found out later that a fourth-year Korean student in our group of eight, named Sin, was a contact point in our school for the uprising. The police really tried to learn things from him—signals, codes, people's names. I insisted that I had no knowledge at all about the plot.

So they tortured me. With my hands tied behind my back, they beat my cheeks, slapped my face, then with a long rod like a baseball bat, they hit me everywhere. The most painful thing was being tied on a long bench, on my back, and then they poured water on my face. When I couldn't breathe, I fainted. Then they revived me. I kept saying I didn't know anything, and they poured it again and it started all over. It lasted two or three hours, and then they started over again.

Some of the others were tortured in different ways—one awful one they called the airplane torture. They take a rope hanging from the ceiling and tie your hands behind your back. Then you stand on a chair, the rope is tied to your hands behind your back and the chair is removed. You are left hanging in the air, and your arms gradually go up and up and up, giving you excruciating pain in your shoulders. I escaped this, but all the others suffered it. After so much of this, time after time, Sin, the leader, finally confessed. Then one by one, the rest of us broke down and confessed. I admitted being part of the network of planning in our school. They detained us about two more months, the eight of us. I was one of three who were not indicted but were released on probation for three years. I was released on June 5, 1934. Six months of my life spent in prison. When I tried to get back into the school, they would not let me in. They told me, however, that since I was a good student, I should try other schools.

Every time I moved my boarding house, from one place to another, invariably within a couple of days the police detective would show up to let me know that he knew I had moved, and that he was watching me. They knew my every movement. Every one.

5 : Through the Eye of a Needle

KANG PYŎNGJU [KANG BYUNG JU]

Bank Manager (m) b. 1910, North P'yŏngan Province

The year the Japanese took over Korea, 1910, is the year I was born, so I never knew life without them. However, the first thing of importance that I remember is the March First Independence Movement in 1919. You may wonder how a child like me at such a young age could get involved in the Independence Movement. It sounds like the claim of Kim Il Sŏng [president of communist North Korea, 1948–1994], who boasted that he was active fighting for Korean independence at an age when most children aren't even aware they have a country.

It happened like this. Chŏngju city was known as the cradle of modernization—it produced active people in many areas. And Tŏktari, our Kang clan village, is only eight kilometers from Chŏngju. In our very own church we had Elder Yi Myŏngnyŏng who became one of the thirty-three signers of the Independence Declaration. Elder Yi lived just over the hill from our village, and of course we knew him and listened to him. Those days, even the villages pulsated with energy and action.

When the Declaration of Independence document was due to arrive in Chŏngju, sometime in March, the people of our area decided to have their own rally in the back stadium of the Osan School. Elder Yi Sŭnghun had suggested the rally—he himself had signed the Declaration representing the Christian churches and also had founded the Osan High School [in 1907; see note 3, chapter 1].

On that day every man of our village got ready to participate, wearing brand-new white clothes. My sister and I—she was thirteen and I was nine—told our parents that we wanted to go with the men. Mother kept saying no, but she gave us new clothes and even put on me a purple vest and black over-jacket. She let us follow the grownups, but the grownups kept telling us to go back, go back. So we followed them at a great distance.

We passed my mother's family home (our maternal grandparents' home) which was about twenty *li* [five miles] from Tŏktari and walked beyond that another ten *li* to where Osan School is located. We each had a Korean flag in our hand—everyone had flags. We waved our flags and people impulsively jumped up to the podium and shouted speeches about the sorrow and anger at losing our country. Somebody handed out pamphlets. I didn't understand them, so I stuffed them in my pockets.

Sister and I shoved our way right into the middle of the grownups. We saw almost no other girls in the crowd, because at the time few women did anything outside their own homes. Shouting and yelling filled the yard. Then, in straight rows, we marched toward Chŏngju station, which is only a short way from the school. We all shouted independence slogans until our voices cracked.

The railroad track coming down from Manchuria and Sinŭiju came through a tunnel just before coming into our station, and that tunnel is right in back of Osan School. The road from the school to the station crosses the tracks. Our parade of demonstrators was just about to cross those tracks when, woooooooo, woooooooooo, a train came out of the tunnel with whistles blowing and stopped right at the intersection in front of the demonstrators. Scores of Japanese soldiers in their brown uniforms jumped out of the train, formed a single line facing the crowd, dropped down on their bellies and started shooting. Tang! Tang! Tang-tang-tang-tang! The gun fire sounded so loud, we froze in terror—but the bullets weren't real. Blanks. They were shooting blanks.

A sexton from our church stood right in front of me and at the first volley of gunshots he fainted. We all wanted to flee but we couldn't leave him lying there, so we shook him and shook him until he came to. Then we all ran away.

Sister and I couldn't very well stop at Grandfather Kim's house—it was a prominent household and the Japanese watched it closely—so we went around that village and up the hill behind it. Sister told me to pull those pamphlets out of my pockets, and we buried them deep in the ground. She said, if we got caught with those things we would be in big trouble. Finally we got home safely.

Change by Choice

After this event there was another gathering for independence in Chŏngju city itself. This time the Japanese responded with firm and ruthless tactics. They shot real bullets and injured many people.

After this, for about ten days, I stayed at home.

GOING TO SCHOOL

In our neighborhood lived Elder Cho Hyŏngjun, a scholar of Chinese classics and character writing. We considered him an "ideologue," meaning he was a visionary opposed to the Japanese rule and working actively to regain independence, both politically and ideologically. He was an educated person and because of this the Japanese military police constantly watched him as a potential threat to their rule.

Since I am the eldest son and therefore should be educated, my father and grandfather took one of the rooms in the outer rim of our Big House [the tile-roof house of the village elder] and converted it into a study room. They invited Elder Cho to be the headmaster to teach me.

Now, the Japanese had just established primary schools in larger towns and cities. One was in Chŏngju city and another was in nearby Napch'ŏn town, where my father practiced medicine.

These schools were still new and we weren't used to them. We heard stories that the teachers were so strict and severe that for punishment they used the most painful of whips made from acacia branches. For even greater punishment, rumor said they put nails through boards and rolled children over them. Of course these stories weren't true. Loyal Koreans circulated them to keep children from going to Japanese schools, all part of the anti-Japanese campaign.

The Japanese ordered county employees to fan out through the villages, round up children and force them to attend primary school. So you can imagine, while we studied Chinese characters in the schoolroom of our house, we kept one eye out watching for the child-catchers. Our room opened up to a clear view of Sŏdang Hill where the officials were likely to appear. Whenever a person with black clothes came down the hill, we all scattered and fled.

Because of all this confusion I never thought of going to primary school; I was perfectly happy with the situation as it was. Strangely enough, my father didn't seem to press me to go there, either. This seemed surprising because he had been one of the first to graduate from the western medical school in Seoul with a Doctor of Medicine degree.

Now about this time, our home studies were interrupted by those Declaration of Independence meetings I told you about. Elder Cho's son, Cho Nakhyŏn, who later became a professor at Yŏnsei University, went to the demonstration, and the Japanese military police shot him in the leg. He limped home and badly needed medical attention, but he knew he'd be arrested if he went to a hospital. His family couldn't go to our house to ask my father to take care of the wounds, since that, too, would lead the police right back to their son. But they got a message to my house, "Please send someone to get your doctor for us," and Mother chose me, thinking that I went back and forth all the time and no one would suspect me. So I went to Napch'ŏn thinking I was only going on an errand.

That day it happened to be raining and Father said, "Yes, I will go back to Mr. Cho and will take care of his wounds, but let us go somewhere together first." I asked him where and he said, "Just follow me."

Huddled under ponchos and umbrellas, we began to walk. To my amazement, our walk ended at the school. A teacher appeared in a resplendent black uniform with gold ornaments on his collar, shoulder, chest, and sleeves, and he wore a saber at his waist. All Japanese government officials wore sabers or swords, and teachers were officials appointed by the Emperor, His Imperial Majesty.

Wouldn't you be frightened out of your wits if you were just ten years old and standing before such a magnificent uniform and long sword? Not only that, he spoke in Japanese, and I did not understand at all. Father said to me, "From today, you will attend primary school. You stay here while I go and take care of Mr. Cho." That is how I started primary school.

After primary school, my father sent me away from my village in the far north to enter the First High School of Kyŏngsŏng [Seoul], where I studied from 1924 to 1928. Nearly all of the students came from primary schools in Seoul. Out of all the hundreds of applicants, the school accepted only three students from the northern Provinces: from South P'yŏngan Province two got in, from North P'yŏngan Province only I made it in, and none at all from Hwanghae Province.

These city kids constantly made fun of us country hicks. When we arrived from the other provinces we had no uniforms; we wore *hanbok*, traditional Korean dress, whereas they came to school in modern attire. My *hanbok* consisted of a long black gown. It is not surprising that they made fun of us, because we really did look odd and out of place.

Yamatomachi, a Japanese street in Pʻyŏngyang, South Pʻyŏngan Province.
All buildings are in Japanese-style architecture, with street name also Japanese, circa 1920.
(Norman Thorpe Collection)

UNIVERSITY LIFE

After completing high school, I planned to attend the university. Grandfather made a strong suggestion that as first son, who would inherit the responsibility of the farms in and around the clan village, I should study agriculture. At that time, if one said *agriculture*, the first school everyone thought of was Hokkaido Imperial University in Japan. This school, founded by an American scholar at the invitation of the Japanese government, was well known for its modern curriculum in agriculture.

I was all set to apply, but my mother strongly opposed it. She was afraid for my safety in Japan because of the Japanese anti-Korean sentiments, partly caused by their mistaken idea that the terrible Kanto earthquake of 1923 was due to the Koreans—many Koreans in Japan were massacred by the Japanese following that earthquake.

So after much thought, I applied to the number one agriculture college in Korea, located in Suwŏn, and attended there from 1929 to 1931.

They said it was like going through the eye of a needle for a Korean to get into the Suwŏn College of Agriculture. The Agriculture Department admitted twenty-five Japanese students and fifteen Koreans each year, and the Forestry Department admitted twenty Japanese and ten Koreans. I graduated at the top of my high school class so I became one of the fifteen Koreans to go through the eye of the needle.

At the college everybody was supposed to live in a dormitory—the West Dorm for the Japanese students and the East Dorm for Koreans. Each dorm was self-governing. For example, for meals in the cafeteria, the food committee hired a cook and purchased food supplies. The library committee purchased books, and both the Japanese and Korean students were supposed to buy identical publications. Each dorm even had its own Ping-Pong committee. So either intentionally or unintentionally, each side did not associate with the other. We studied together in class and did laboratory experiments together, but we seldom compared notes or talked to each other. Usually we just nodded to acknowledge the other's presence. This is the kind of symbiotic relationship we had with the Japanese students.

Many teachers at this school had been very active in the Independence Movement. One faculty member went to North Korea after the Japanese were driven out at the end of the Second World War and became a Cabinet Minister in the Kim Il Sŏng communist government.

So you see, going through the Agriculture College put us in such an elite group that most of the graduates became headmasters of schools and bank managers. That is attributable in no small measure to the Confucian reverence for learning.

About three years before I entered, an incident took place at the college. Some of the Korean students decided to teach the farm children how to read and write. They also taught Korean history. These children wrote compositions, and in them wrote sentences implying a desire for Korean independence. Unfortunately, this was discovered by Japanese secret police detectives and caused an uproar.

The Korean students also organized a group called *Kaech'ŏk sa* (Agriculture Development Association). After graduation, they planned to devote their time and energy to teaching Korean farmers the most modern farming techniques. They were passionate idealists dedicated to the welfare and improvement of Korean farmers. They were willing to sacrifice their high social status with its future leadership roles and money for this ideal. The association planned to build a demonstration farm in Kangwŏn-do, where land was cheaper and hitherto uncultivated. They wanted to invite some tenant farmers to live on this farm and actually experience modern farming methods.

Well, it wasn't to be. The Japanese police had become very sensitive and watchful of any group activity on the part of Korean students. They especially watched for anything that sounded like independence activities, especially among the leadership class of Korea which was then in college. They got wind of this agriculture development group, and harassed the members by jailing them, expelling them from the college, and, in effect, disbanding the group. [See chapter 7 for Mr. Kim's part in these activities.]

In my third year, my last year at the college, the students elected me president of the dorm. Although we had our own dormitory and took care of our own governing rules and everyday living, including food, this year the Japanese decided to act out their slogan that "Japan and Korea are one" by mixing the Korean and Japanese students in the dormitory.

Since there were many more of them than us, the school officials told us that each room would have two or three Japanese students and one Korean student. We Korean students protested vehemently, and the officials finally compromised by allowing each room to be composed of one nationality or the other, but side by side. We even protested that. Finally they said, all right, we'll alternate each hall, so every other hall will be occupied by one nationality.

Throughout all this controversy and conflict, I moved back and forth between the Japanese officials and the Korean students. It was not an easy task but finally it was resolved. We gave in on two things. First, we agreed to share the same library with the Japanese students, and second, we agreed to bathe in the same bathroom. The bathing was required every day because we returned from the farm laboratory hot, tired, and dirty.

In all those three years, though we studied side by side, we never socialized together. The separation between Japanese and Korean students remained thorough and complete.

RETURN TO THE FAR NORTH AS A BANK MANAGER

I finished college in 1932 and needed a job. I heard that the Japanese government was recruiting managers for the Bank of Agriculture, and had decided to allow Koreans to apply. This was unusual, because the current managers were all Japanese as part of Japan's long-range plan to manage and control the farming in Korea.

The bank planned to select forty people—thirty Japanese and ten Koreans. So regardless of how qualified the Koreans might be, only ten could expect jobs. And though unqualified, thirty Japanese would be chosen. More than a thousand Koreans applied. I decided to apply.

I ranked as one of the ten Koreans selected and began an orientation course. After an accounting class in Seoul came field training in the provinces. I spent two months in North P'yŏngan Province, two months of class work and orientation in Seoul, four months in Sinŭiju right on the Yalu River, and another three months in Huch'ang, a remote city at the northern end of North P'yŏngan Province.

The base salary of a government position for a graduate of a Japanese public college was fifty-five yen a month and for graduates of private colleges (Korean or missionary) it was forty-five yen. By comparison, the county chief got sixty yen, the police chief got thirty, regular civil servants got fifteen, and policemen got only eight.

People assigned to remote areas of the provinces received an extra hardship bonus equivalent to 30 percent of their salary. Also, those living near the northern border, along the Yalu or Tuman rivers, received another seven yen. The salaries for both Japanese and Korean bank managers appeared to be the same, but the Japanese received still another extra 30 percent stipend.

My first permanent assignment was at the Bank of Agriculture in Hǔich'ǒn. My salary was 55 yen plus a 10-yen discretionary fund plus the 30 percent "hardship allowance," so it added up to 81.50 yen, which in those days was a very, very generous salary for a young man who was only twenty three or twenty-four years old. [In 1930, one month living in a boarding house cost 25 yen.]

Between my wife and me (this is before any of our children were born), we couldn't possibly spend that much money. Our cost of living amounted to only about 10 yen a month. We spent nothing on entertainment—no entertainment existed in that remote, rural location. So you see how much money we could save. We simply had no place to spend it.

What did I do with the money? I spent it on books, books, and more books. Every time we moved, the books were so heavy and occupied so much space that it gave me a headache! But a worthwhile headache. Also we bought an organ. I remember that organ! Pumping it. Can you imag-

Change by Choice

ine? Usually the church had one, or the school, but we had one in our own home. A good one. So we lived pretty well, and kept busy.

The bank transferred me to Chŏnch'ŏn, still in North P'yŏngan Province, in 1941, the year [the United States officially joined] the Second World War. The Japanese officials there had became rather complacent and tolerant toward Koreans. Also the town, although big, was quite out of the way. So both publicly in my job, and privately with my family, life there was most pleasant.

Nearly everything was rationed in those days, even in our peaceful, remote corner. Rice, clothing, cloth, liquor—everything. But while we lived in Chŏnch'ŏn (1941–1944) we managed not to be short of anything because we had a family friend, also named Kang. A very wealthy man. He helped us. He gave gifts to the Japanese to placate them, so they allowed him to keep his wealth.

MAKING COLD NOODLES

Winters were harsh that far north, and there weren't many outside activities because of the weather. What I remember most is the women getting together to make *naeng myŏn* (cold noodles). We made everything from scratch. We made the dough. We made the noodles. We plucked the pheasant. We got the condiments. All that work, to eat it as a special nightcap served after several rounds of *hwat'u* (a card game).

To make the noodles we had to squeeze the dough through small holes at the bottom of a contraption—a noodle press—and the noodles fell directly into boiling water in the pot below. The press was something like a piston. To add weight to push the dough through, I would actually stand on the contraption, and it would slowly sink down. Sometimes, when it was going slowly, I would pick up my young son and hold him, to add more weight to push the noodles through into the boiling water.

You might wonder how we got all the good foods needed for the *naeng myŏn*, since it was during the war and food was rationed. Well, there were shortages of course, and things did get worse toward the end of the war, but they were still bearable. Also the police overlooked enforcing some of the rationing rules because of the other Mr. Kang. Was it bribery? I never really knew what he did, but we all benefited. Much later we heard that on the very day the Japanese surrendered, the Koreans turned against him, attacked and beat him, calling him a Japanese sympathizer. He barely escaped with his life. We did not see this, for by then we had moved on to another town.

A UNIQUE LEADERSHIP ROLE

All across Korea, the Japanese government increasingly tried to unify the attitude of its citizens, especially those in leadership positions. They used the slogan "One Body, One Spirit."

In order for everyone in town to actually see a tangible demonstration of our unity, the Japanese commanded all community leaders to take part in the early morning calisthenics. If they didn't, they suffered greatly for it. Only the leaders had to do this, so in the bank I had to attend, but no one else. Every morning early we would gather at the school grounds and engage in calisthenics. They called it "Spiritual Training and Exercise." By spiritual, they meant their Shintoism, which in simple terms is nothing but shamanism.

Another ritual to increase our spiritual training consisted of immersing our bodies in the river early in the morning—summer and winter. In winter we had to break the ice to dunk ourselves in. Then we must hold hands and chant the names of the many gods of Japan—and there are about eight million of them. It took thirty minutes in the water—bitter cold near Siberia, winter wind coming down—oh, it was unbearable in the winter.

On these mornings we also lined up on the riverbank and exercised. Not ordinary calisthenics. We worked our way through specially developed Shinto body movements called, in Japanese, *Misogi Harai*. Literally, this means warding off the evil spirits and at the same time worshipping and praising those spirits that protect and give prosperity.

Now remember, all the leaders in high position, school principals and so forth, all these other leaders except for me were all Japanese. Many of these Japanese leaders did not know the rituals or how to do them. In fact, only three people knew the rituals because of their higher education and background. These three were the police chief, the elementary school principal—and me. But the police chief couldn't always come because of police matters, so the principal and I alternated in supervising this ritual.

Mr. Kang's son interrupted, saying, "Father was more highly educated than any of these Japanese leaders. The Japanese leaders realized that and respected him for it. I remember, when I was eight or nine years old, that the Japanese police chief,

*the most powerful man in town, always bowed low to my father. At the time I
didn't know why, but it impressed me, even then."*

Among the friends that I got to know well because of our official contacts were the medical doctor (a Korean) and the police chief (a Japanese).
The police station stood right across the street from the bank and our
house—the bank manager's job always included a residence right next to
the bank. Because of the proximity of the police station and the bank, we
got together often to play *paduk* ["go" in Japanese, a type of board game
using black and white stones]. So you might say we became friends—as
close as a Japanese and a Korean could come in those days.

That "One Body, One Spirit" slogan did not fool us, however! It sounded
good on paper. Supposedly it meant that we, both Japanese and Koreans,
were all children of the Divine Emperor and therefore should be treated
equally. But actually, the Japanese desperately wanted to find ways to use
Korean manpower, especially men from age eighteen to about forty, for
their military use—by now many of their own men had been killed in the
war. So we were not fooled. They wanted us to carry out their war effort.

They didn't want to give Koreans guns to fight side by side with them
because they didn't trust us. So they put Koreans into the menial jobs to
free the Japanese to go as soldiers. *Ching yong* (labor draft) is noncombat
work, and they drafted men into this service to do assembly-line work
making parts for airplanes, tanks, and military supplies, and to work in the
mines—all this to relieve Japanese men to do the actual fighting.

Then came *ching byŏng* (military draft) toward the end of the war. The
Japanese ran out of their own men entirely and had to make soldiers out of
Koreans. They had to give us guns; they desperately needed bodies to go to
the front.

During this time, my family moved away from Chŏnch'ŏn.

I EARN A DEMOTION

As the war intensified, the Japanese management became increasingly para-
noid. I was promoted to the bank branch in the city of Kanggye, then demoted to the remote city of Pyŏktong, a hydroelectric boomtown far up
the Yalu River. What I did to merit such a drastic demotion was to take an
unauthorized trip that the Japanese considered to be highly irregular. I
started from Huch'ang and went through Hamgyŏng Province through

Hŭich'ŏn and returned. You must remember that this was near the end of the war and the Japanese were nervous because they were about to lose the war, so when I got back they met me with a demotion and transferred me to a bank in the town of Pyŏktong.

Pyŏktong was truly remote. To get to that town, upstream from the dam, we took a tiny riverboat and spent all day, eight hours, putt-putting slowly upriver. This town was so remote I expected it to be quite terrible, and yet the mountains, the hills, and the river were beautiful, and when I heard a boat whistle in the distance I was overcome with the serenity of it all. Even if you weren't a poet, you would start composing poems. It was there we greeted the liberation of Korea in August 1945.

The places we lived—Kanggye, Chŏnch'ŏn, Sinp'ung—these places, though rural, were full of natural beauty. I look at these sojourns, paid for by the bank over the years, as free sightseeing tours. In that sense it was not a wasted experience but rather an opportunity for which we thank the Lord.

AN ELUSIVE DREAM—1945

Once the war was over and the Japanese left, we returned to our hometown of Chŏngju and I became bank manager there. Everyone expected that Koreans finally would regain their independence and self-respect.

I remained cautious, waiting to see what happened next. Less than a year later, in 1946, the new communist regime disbanded the Bank of Agriculture and started the so-called Agriculture Association. [To be a manager in the new association, one had to join the Communist Party, which Mr. Kang refused to do.] I resigned my post.

EPILOGUE, 1945–1986

Mr. Kang quietly moved to South Korea in February 1947 to escape the communists, and two months later his wife and five children secretly escaped in a fishing boat and joined him in Seoul. He managed banks in several southern cities, and survived the Korean War in the small town of Mulgŭm not far from Pusan, adding child number six to the family. When peace returned, he bought a bit of land in the Anyang vineyards near Seoul, and from there guided all six of his children through college. Eventually, five of the six children emigrated to the United States. The elder Kangs visited America, where Mrs. Kang died of illness in 1971 while living with their son's family in New York. Mr. Kang returned to Korea and died there in 1986.

6 : Business Ventures and Adventures

Tradition holds that sons follow in the professions of their fathers, but Koreans, especially during the 1920s, found more and more choices open to them. Under the new "cultural" rule (period of accommodation, 1920–1931), the Japanese continued to restrict, but did not entirely block, Korean entrepreneurship. The stories that follow give voice to this wider range of options.

Life was especially hard for farmers, who often lived at subsistence level. The first two informants recall this poverty. Other young men put forth great effort to learn skills and find new jobs, many of which put them in varying degrees of contact with the Japanese. We asked the elders if they saw this as "collaboration," and found that each had a clear gut-level distinction between individuals who had actively aided the Japanese and those who simply made use of situations to survive and possibly even flourish. Some seize the moment and rise, and would have risen in any situation. Bruce Cumings puts their feelings into words when he says, "What was the alternative for talented Koreans in this colony? To miss their life chances through renunciation, to resist and end up dead or in jail, or to participate."[1]

YI CHAE'IM, (f) b. 1919, housewife, Kyŏnggi Province:
I married at nineteen to a farmer, and was so busy trying to survive on our little farm that I had no time to think of anything else. I didn't worry about the Japanese. All my learning disappeared. I really suffered. I had a hard, hard life and nearly died of such hard work.

SIN KWANGSŎNG, (m) b. 1915, farmer, North Kyŏngsang Province:
One thing I remember. Inside the thatch roof, when it decays, there are a lot of bugs, and they are an off-white color and they smell. Well, one day I was making soup and these bugs fell in. It was so disgusting, I almost threw up. But when you are so hungry, what can you do? We just dug them out and ate the rest of the soup. When I had my bowl, one was still in it. I dug it out and finished the whole bowl. We were that poor, we couldn't throw out that disgusting soup. Now I can laugh about it, but it shows you how poor we were.

KIM SUNOK, (m) b. 1910, peddler/fireman, Kyŏnggi Province:
Map'o, near Seoul, was just a village when I lived there. My family was once high class—ya, my seventeenth ancestor, Kim Chongsŏ, was a vice prime minister and a general around 1450. But I know nothing about my grandfather or other ancestors. Aigo! I had no time to learn about them. All my time was spent trying to survive.

My mother, she died when I was seven, and when I was ten (1920) I got into business for myself. I went to Namdae-mun market in Seoul, bought fruit, carried it back to Map'o, set it on a mat on the street, and sold it at a higher price. In winter I bought dried fish on a skewer. I couldn't sit with them on the street—too cold. I sold them from shop to shop. I did this for about five years until I was fifteen.

I did all sorts of sports with the neighborhood boys—yeah, weightlifting, parallel bars, and baseball. I was pretty good in weightlifting so I got to have strong muscles. The other boys spoke Japanese, so I yelled at them, saying, "Do you like the Japanese? How could you? Don't speak Japanese in front of me."

But, listen to this. As I got older, I got to thinking that although I hated the Japanese, I gotta speak their language. As the old saying goes, you know, "To capture the tiger, you gotta go into the tiger's cave." So I bought a book and taught myself the basic phrases. How about that!

Near Yongsan station was a railroad factory where they made engine parts, and many Koreans, like about three thousand, worked there. Each department had a sports team; haha—they hired people to play sports, and not work! That's what I did. The athlete guys all told me that I was stronger than they were, so they nicknamed me "Ox." Of the three thousand workers, about a hundred were sport guys. We were all Korean, but

Change by Choice

the coaches were Japanese and they spoke to us only in Japanese. Well, that's how I got to speak better Japanese.

After a while I got restless and left the factory. I got into rice dealing, hair cutting, wine selling, then fruit selling. I tried many things, 'cause I really had no skills myself. I just hired other guys when I needed them. If one job didn't work out, I changed to something else, you know. My businesses took me all over the northern half of Korea, even to Manchuria! Boy, that was exciting! I would visit these places, do business, and move on.

When I was about twenty-four, people began asking me why I didn't get married. I told them, "Aigo! I am just too poor." But one day my friend said he knew a woman who could get me a nice bride, and my father said, "Well, why don't we look into that? If we like her, we can come up with some money for a marriage."

The go-between said we should at least go meet the bride. So off we went to her place, a small three-room house with a tiny courtyard. The girl had her back toward me and wouldn't turn around, can you believe that? I couldn't find out what she looked like. She was only twelve, but we decided to go ahead. Two weeks later we exchanged gifts, and after a month we had an official wedding. Come to think of it, looking back, it was comical!

Boy, if I start talking there is no end. I am an antique, an old relic, but now I want to tell you about my father.

My father eked out his living as a *chige* (A-frame backpack) carrier. He still wore his hair in a topknot, even with the Japanese running the country. Ah, I felt so bad for my father, carrying things on his back all day, I just couldn't bear to see him working so hard. You know what I did? After I got married, I tell you, the first thing I did was to take his *chige*, smash it to pieces, and have him live with me and my new bride. We served him until his death, five years later. It made me so sad when he died.

Because of my strength, the local fire station recruited me to work there. I was made second in charge of the Map'o station from 1938 until 1945. When the Japanese started the forced draft, the Japanese fire chief guy said, "I may send everybody else off to the war, but not you. You are needed here." Ha! The reason was that I always took first place at the firefighting competition held twice a year at Yongsan Middle School grounds. I always brought back certificates and awards, and my boss liked those things.

I have many more stories to tell. I had seven life-and-death crises, and I'm still here alive. Come back again and I'll tell you all of them.

PAK C. [ANONYMOUS], (f) b. 1927, housewife:

Remember, I attended an all-Japanese school in Seoul? My stay there lasted only one year, and after that I returned to my family in P'yŏngyang. I was allowed into that school because, as a textile merchant, my father had lots of contact with Japanese businessmen. Father had yards and yards of fabrics, because he bought textiles from the Japanese and sold to Korean retailers. Because of his business in P'yŏngyang, he often traveled to Japan. Sometimes we received gifts from the Japanese businessmen. I remember once receiving a whole crate of oranges from a businessman in Yamaguchi prefecture, Japan.

My father even owned a horse. It was an expensive hobby, but his business was good enough to enable him to have it. I remember him dressed in very fashionable clothes, with bow tie, flaring pants, and boots. He looked so handsome. Because the Japanese in P'yŏngyang had a battalion of mounted police, my father paid a monthly fee and stabled his horse with theirs. He even got friendly with the Japanese mounted police because of their common interest in horses.

I don't remember any harassment by the Japanese police or government officials, because, I suppose, my father had to be on good terms with them, otherwise he'd be out of business. If he was stressed by this, I was too young to notice.

KIM P. [ANONYMOUS], (f) b. 1931, housewife:

My family moved to Seoul from a small farming village near Andong. My father didn't want to work on the farm, so he left by secretly selling a cow. He used the money to go to Japan to learn a trade and he returned a carpenter.

I was one of the only Korean girls to attend a Japanese school, and it was because my father got a job as carpenter in charge of maintenance for the Japanese hospital in the eastern outskirts of Seoul. They called it a sanitarium; I guess it had mostly tuberculosis patients. Father maintained the buildings and built storage sheds. He took care of the wards as well as the living quarters for the staff.

Because father worked on the hospital grounds, they gave us housing right among the Japanese hospital staff. We each had our own little garden and some of the things we grew, we exchanged with our neighbors. Whenever the staff members needed something fixed, my father did it for them.

So every time they went to Japan, they brought back presents to father and our whole family. I really didn't feel any discrimination.

PAK SŎNGP'IL,
(m) b. 1917, farmer/fisherman, South Kyŏngsang Province:
When I was a young man, I made a rather brazen decision that affected my entire life. I lived in a village of about two hundred houses, right at the seashore, so that people there were mostly fishermen. My own family, however, owned a large farm, with rice paddies, vegetable plots, and woods. We had many helpers to farm such a large amount. During my grandfather's time, our property was even larger, but Grandfather sold off much of the land to come up with money for my aunt's trial. [See chapter 2.]

Grandfather had a high government position under the old monarchy, and he kept it when the Japanese arrived. His position was called *ch'ambong*, so people always called him Pak Ch'ambong, even long after he had left office. They called me Pak Ch'ambong's grandson. When the Japanese organized the administrative districts, my grandfather was appointed head of the township (*myŏn*) of Kijang. You might call our family prominent in our own area. [Note: The official rank of the *ch'ambong* position was number nine, the lowest in the civil service system. However, passing the *kwagŏ* (civil service exam) and receiving any government title at all did confer status locally, as is seen here in the villagers' esteem of Mr. Pak.]

I went through six years of primary school, and then in 1937, when I was about twenty, I began working for a local sardine fishing association. First I had a desk job, but I soon found that the fishermen made the same pay for one night's work that I was getting for a whole month. So I told myself, this is not good. I better get into fishing.

Now, you realize, I did not know the first thing about fishing, so I was rather brash. I just went out and bought myself a fishing boat with an engine, and, just like sailing in a breeze in smooth waters, I started making money hand over fist. Business boomed. Catching was excellent.

With one boat I learned all I needed to know about running a boat. As for how to cast nets and catch the fish, I hired skilled crewmen. Soon I owned three boats. In those days, owning *three* boats put me in the affluent class. When I came back after a night out catching huge amounts of fish, all three boats full, the people said, "What a successful young man!" They said I was very diligent and whatever I touched, prospered. They'd say, "You know, he's the grandson of that important Pak Ch'ambong." I tell you, I was an industrious person—I never sat still. For example, there is a sardine season and an off-season. While other fishermen took it easy during the off season, I still used my boats and went out to sea. All summer we transported seaweed from Kijang to Pusan and that brought in lots of money. We also used the boats to carry other things, and people paid me for the freight.

Trouble began when the Second World War started. I needed heavy oil to run those engines, but the Japanese cut off all oil to private business. I simply could not run my boats. Besides, the men who worked on my crews were all drafted to the South Seas by the Japanese army.

Then an interesting thing happened. I was spared. The Japanese army brought their huge transport ships into Pusan harbor to take troops to the South Seas, but first, the soldiers had to be given physical exams. Well, there I was, so the Japanese navy appropriated me and one of my boats. My job was to ferry ten doctors out to the transport ship every morning, wait while they went aboard ship, examined the men and came back down. Then I ferried them back to shore. They took my boat, but they paid me for the job.

Here is how my own trouble started. Remember, my family had a large farm. Well, the Japanese took 70 percent of our crops and we kept only 30 percent. We thought that was way too much, so my family and others who owned their farms got together and had a meeting. The police representative came, and we demanded that they lower the tax. We said, "How can you expect us to survive when you take away practically everything that we make!" We tried to reason with them, and I spoke up, apparently too loudly, because the next day I was dragged to the police station and beat up so badly I thought I was going to die. Because of that, and also because of my aunt's being an anti-Japanese activist, they now considered me a politically dangerous person and watched me closely all the time.

Later I got beat up many times by the Japanese because I resisted changing my name to Japanese.

KIM WŎN'GŬK [KIM WON KEUK],
·(m) b. 1918, Tobacco Authority officer, North Hamgyŏng Province:
After I graduated from trade high school in 1938, I got a job with the Tobacco Authority. They hired only two Koreans that year, and I was one of them.

I worked in a branch office of the Morphine Bureau in South Hamgyŏng Province (our main office was up in North Hamgyŏng). This bureau had a deceptive name, Plant Analysis Bureau—it really dealt with opium.

Everyone who worked there had to be trustworthy because opium was illegal, and the Japanese kept a close eye on this toxic medicine. They trusted me enough to give me the key to the storeroom where they kept the drugs. My superior, a Japanese, said, "Young Mr. Kaneda (my Japanese name), I tend to misplace keys, so why don't you take care of them for me during the day?"

They had several official opium farms. They harvested it, analyzed it, and produced morphine. One farm was in North Hamgyŏng, where the soil was right for it. Wherever the opium was cultivated, if the authorities detected any misbehavior from the villagers around the opium farm, then they punished the entire village and evacuated it. I knew absolutely nothing about what happened to it [the opium] after it left us. Later we heard that most of it was sent to Manchuria to ease the pain of Japanese soldiers in the army hospitals.

I am not really a very talented person, not very articulate or outgoing. I am just an honest, diligent man. When the Japanese realized that, they treated me fairly. In about four or five years, I was promoted four times, and got a raise each time. So I must say, I was treated the same as my Japanese coworkers and not discriminated against.

KIM SANGSUN, (m) b. 1916, miner/truck driver, Kyŏnggi Province:
When I was young I dreamed of being a bus driver! A highway passed through our village right in front of our school. On it, the buses went by— you could see them from the classroom. The drivers looked so stylish and glamorous, to my childish eyes that I wanted to become like them.

At seventeen I graduated from primary school, and right away I begged my grandfather for permission to become a bus driver. What I got instead was a severe beating with grandfather's long pipe, and a lecture that no grandson of a *yangban* (upper class) should have such a low-class job.

I was full of energy, already full-grown and I looked like an adult, so I left home to make my way in the world. I went to North Ch'ungch'ŏng Province to find work in a gold mine.

Yes, it was owned and operated by the Japanese, with many Japanese working there, all the way from the chief down to the workers. There was all sorts of gold, in the riverbeds among the sand or mixed with rocks in the mountain, but I didn't want to work in the mines. I looked around. I noticed there was no electricity except for their own ten-horsepower generator. I decided I wanted to operate that equipment. Back home we had a four horsepower rice machine, so I knew I liked working with machines.

I went up to the Korean who operated the generator, and asked him to teach me. He said he'd have to teach me in secret when the Japanese chief wasn't looking. In fact, he told me that in my application I must say I already had that skill, rather than that I wanted to learn. He pointed to a hill a little distance away and told me to hide there and watch until he signaled me.

Whenever the chief wasn't around I went down and got training from that Korean worker. I remembered everything he told me. He was impressed, and indeed, I got the job three months later, hired by the Japanese.

About 1937, my uncle spoke to me about starting a business trucking food from our village farms into Seoul to sell it for a profit. Finally I had a reason to get my driving license, but we soon found out that it was next to impossible for civilians to run their own trucking business. Japan had started the war with China and had taken all available trucks to the front. On top of that, because of the war, there was severe gasoline rationing. Well, without gasoline, you cannot run a truck, even if you have one. So now I had a license, but no truck.

You must remember that at this time young men were being drafted, and I wanted to avoid that. I thought and thought. I knew someone who worked for the Chŏnnam Railroad Company and I got a job driving trucks for them. People were very kind, and I liked it there. In the surrounding area were many tobacco fields, so tobacco is what I carried. Each trip was a day trip only. I always came home at night.

With the Second World War raging and a shortage of gasoline, our trucks were outfitted with wood-burning engines. These engines coughed and sputtered, so we couldn't go fast. Not only that, but burning wood produced lots of soot, so we looked filthy! We wore overalls while we drove, and carried along a dress shirt to wear at night when we went to restaurants to drink and be merry.

I don't mean to brag, but I was a good mechanic. Just to get a license in

Change by Choice

those days, you had to know how to do your own repairs. Repair shops didn't exist.

Since Yesan was a large market city, whenever I delivered something out to the small towns, invariably I picked up something to bring back, such as persimmons, fruits, onions, garlic—you name it. I got things cheap, and then ate them or sold them. Once in a while I brought people back in the truck and they paid me, but of course this was against all rules.

I know I wasn't the only one using the truck this way, because the railroad hired private detectives with hunting rifles to lie in wait among the trees, stop the trucks, and make spot checks. It was easy for them to catch us with so few trucks on the road. So we often drove in fear. In spite of that, my life was good. I thought it would continue forever.

Now it happened that my fellow truck driver was a Japanese named Sumida. One day in early summer, he asked me, "Do you plan to stay with this company for a long time?"

"I have no other plans because if I quit, I will be drafted," I said.

He whispered to me that in a few days he planned to vanish, and he suggested that I do the same.

"Think of it," he said. "When an egg fights with a rock, who do you think will win? Rock, of course. [China is the rock.] And Japan is the egg. We have exhausted all our materials to fight this war. Our days are numbered. I suggest that you go into hiding somewhere, to protect yourself."

Indeed, a few days later, he disappeared. So I said to myself, he usually has accurate information. If he made such a drastic move, things must be really dire. I submitted my resignation and sure enough, within three months the war was over—the Japanese occupation finished.

CH'OE P'ANBANG,
(m) b. 1912, Morse code operator, North Kyŏngsang Province:
I had plenty of contact with the Japanese. My job was as a Morse code operator, and in order to collect the intelligence information, police came regularly to my office.

It took me about a year to get my code license. At the training school, they chose fifty Japanese and only thirty Koreans. They always ran short of the fifty and never filled those slots, but the number of Korean applicants was well over a thousand, more like fifteen hundred for those thirty slots. Somehow I got in.

Once we passed the test, everybody got jobs with the Ministry of Communication. We worked day and night, twenty-four-hour shifts to keep the wireless functioning. Then we got twenty-four hours off.

We Koreans felt plenty of discrimination. First, our salary was lower for doing the same job. Second, they got a housing allowance and hardship assistance. Third, all public agencies had a kitchen and a place to sleep, so that two people could stay overnight, taking turns. We Koreans pulled much more than our fair share of this overnight duty. Fourth, Japanese workers got rapid promotions, while it took us much, much longer to get promoted. I really didn't like it. How could I feel good about such treatment? There was just no remedy. None.

I did become friends with some Japanese. We'd go out and drink together. Even after the liberation, we exchanged some letters. I have to admit, on an individual level, some Japanese are good people.

At my job, all military information came through the wire. The movement of troops; when units were scheduled to arrive in Taegu—I heard it all. One thing we had going for us was that the military police depended on us for hard intelligence, so they treated us with kid gloves. I heard all things. Everything passed my desk.

Toward the end of the war, when they were drafting Koreans into the army, we were spared because they considered our jobs essential for the war effort.

YANG SŎNGDŎK,
(m) b. 1919, electrical engineer, South Ch'ungch'ŏng Province:
I attended a technical school in Seoul and became an electrical engineer. I can give you one example after another of Japanese discrimination.

Suppose a Japanese merchant and a Korean merchant apply for a permit to open stores in the same neighborhood, and they apply on the same day. The next day, the Japanese gets his permit and proceeds to open his store. The Korean merchant goes every day to get his permit. One month, two months go by. By that time, even a Buddha will run out of patience. Finally he gets the permit, but by then the Japanese store is established and is a going concern. Naturally, the Korean cannot keep up. Such discrimination was rampant.

Another example of such treatment is that when we engineers were assigned as apprentices to the actual electrical stations around Korea, all the

The large rice export center at Kunsan, North Chŏlla Province on Korea's southwest coast, where rice is being prepared for shipment to Japan, circa 1920. (Norman Thorpe Collection)

choice locations went to the Japanese. Koreans got sent to far-away rural areas and had to make do with antiquated equipment. They assigned me to a remote power station up in the Kanggye area of North P'yŏngan Province, near the Manchurian border. At night we could see lights flickering across the Yalu River in Manchuria. Rumor said that those lights came from bands of roving Korean guerrilla fighters.

The company wanted to send workers to China, but none of the Japanese wanted to go because China was a war zone. So I volunteered because it counted as war effort and I could get deferment from the draft. I went to China shortly after the great Nanking massacre of 1937, and with my own eyes I saw corpses piled high on the streets, corpses blocking sewers, and absolutely brutal bayonet practices. But that's a different story. You asked about life in Korea.

SONG SŎKCHI, (m) b. 1916, leather merchant, Kyŏnggi Province:

After high school, I went into the leather business and stayed in that business until the Second World War started. The Japanese did not get into the leather business, as it was beneath their dignity, so I had no competition from them. I purchased sheets of leather wholesale from Japan and sold them to Koreans who made shoes, briefcases, and suitcases. The bulk of our business was by mail order. We sent merchandise to distant places, even Manchuria.

As the war dragged on, it became difficult to get material, so we dealers got together and formed an association to share the remaining supplies. Soon Japan banned the use of leather altogether and began manufacturing imitation leather by compacting layers and layers of newspaper. Even this came from Japan.

There was a black market, so on the side we bought leather goods that somehow got in from Japan. The Japanese police quickly noticed that people still wore leather, and they began posing as customers to buy things and then arrest the shopkeepers.

I had a contact person up north in Hamgyŏng Province with whom I had many dealings over the years. He called to say he had a new customer who wanted to buy genuine leather. Since I had known my contact for a long time, and trusted him, I said all right. I collected several weeks' worth of leather from our co-op and sold it to the new man.

The next thing I knew, two police detectives entered our store and asked for me by name. My heart sank, I was so frightened! I couldn't think of anything that I had done to cause them to come for me.

They took out a piece of paper with a name on it and asked me if I knew that person, and I saw the name of the person my friend had introduced to me. That man already had been arrested.

These detectives had come all the way from P'yŏngyang to arrest me. They worked for a nationwide police network called Economic Crimes. They could show up anywhere. My store was under the jurisdiction of the police in Seoul, but these detectives did not even notify the local police. They took me by train all the way north to P'yŏngyang. I said I'd like to call home first, to tell my family. They said, "We will tell them soon enough. Let's go."

They questioned me that very evening, and put me in a holding cell. I was devastated. Periodically they took me out of my cell to the interrogation room and asked where the leather came from. They wanted to find out who the black marketeers were in Japan. I told them that I didn't buy it from dealers in Japan, but from some intermediary.

They never did contact my family. Witnesses saw me being taken and they told my family. All they knew was that the police took me away. They had no idea where I was.

My eldest brother was head of Chong-no Public Library in Seoul. He found out where I was and came to see me. The police made him write a promissory note to guarantee that I would not flee. Brother also brought clean clothes for me. I went to the barber shop to clean up, and returned to Seoul.

CH'OE KILSŎNG, (m) b. 1911, teacher, Kyŏnggi Province:

My life began in an orderly fashion in Map'o, near Seoul. I went through school, obtained my teacher's license, and began teaching in Ŭijŏngbu, northeast of Seoul. Then life became complicated.

I got demoted to a small primary school in remote Ansŏng county, Ilchuk township. If I had been clever, this would not have happened, but I wasn't very street smart. I rubbed the Japanese higher-ups the wrong way. I claimed that there are Korean words that Japanese words cannot match — there are no equivalent words in Japanese. They did not like to hear that.

I taught there in Ilchuk for four years, and then they demoted me again, this time to an island school in Puch'ŏng-gun, Yŏhŭng township. The Japanese considered me a deviant, a maverick — to put it nicely, a nonconformist. If I had gone along with them, this would not have happened, but somehow I just didn't play along with their games.

I took my whole family out to the island. There on the island, there was just the Japanese principal and me to run the school. We had about one hundred students. Grades one and two were together in one classroom and grades three and four worked together in another. After a while, a Korean principal came to the island. Did he come because he wanted to? Who would want to!

Exile to an island was supposed to last only three years, and then you got returned to the mainland. But even there, I managed to rub them the wrong way. I really don't know how we disagreed so often. I'd say something the principal didn't like, and I wouldn't let go. Then he said insulting things to me. They extended my exile. I stayed there six years. It was hilarious—it had never happened before, such a long exile.

Somehow, from the island, I got returned all the way to Seoul. I did not ask for the transfer. A notice came to transfer me to the Sokongduk Primary School, and I taught there until the end of the Japanese rule.

A persistent hostile feeling always surged inside me, about the Japanese being our overlords. I always felt resentful toward them. That colored all my actions, and it showed up in my demotions and exiles. I never did any specific anti-Japanese activities, I just talked back to insults when I should have kept silent. To survive, most people went along with the insults, humiliation, and persecution. It really hurt our emotions.

7 : I Almost Went to Canada

YI OKHYŎN

Housewife (f) b. 1911, North P'yŏngan Province

KIM CHANDO

Teacher-turned-Farmer (m) b. 1907, Hwanghae Province

Mr. Kim died of illness in San Francisco shortly before the interviews began. His wife, Ms. Yi, tells their story.

In order to avoid the wars, Grandfather settled in a small village near the Yalu River, bought land, and became prominent in the community. As prosperous farmers, we became self-supporting, slaughtered our own pigs and chickens, and raised all our own food.

Father, being second son, was free to leave the farm, so he attended the Presbyterian theological seminary in P'yŏngyang for four years. I went to high school in the city.

You know that girls sometime get love letters from boys, don't you? In P'yŏngyang high school I kept getting letters like that, and it worried my parents. They were very concerned that it was unsafe, so I think they wanted to see me safely married. The school built an auditorium and in the opening ceremonies I sang solos twice, one in the afternoon and one in the evening. So naturally, everyone got to know my name and who I was. That's how, I think, all those letters came.

After Father graduated from seminary, his first pastorate was at a church in Hwanghae Province, and later he moved to pastor a church in Wŏnsan, a huge port on the Eastern Sea. To keep the family together, I transferred to Wŏnsan Girls' High School, run by Canadian Methodist missionaries, for my last year of school. I arrived just in time for some excitement.

You remember the Kwangju student incident in 1929? [*See chapter 4.*] Well, shortly before we graduated in March 1930, my classmates and I decided to demonstrate, shout *mansei*, in sympathy with those Kwangju students—after all, we were fellow students. First on the school grounds, and then, two here, three there, we all left school and converged outside and started going down the street.

One of my classmates disguised herself as a peasant by changing into Korean dress (*hanbok*) with a scarf over her head, and she guarded the alley. The rest of us wore our school uniforms and surged forward to the street. The next thing we knew, the Japanese police came and rounded us up.

The police didn't know what to do with us. They couldn't very well put us girls in the regular prison, so they herded us to their battalion headquarters and pushed us into their martial arts practice building, a big building with a wooden floor and high windows—a huge, bare room. They used one corner of the room for Japanese sword practice and the other side for judo. None of us felt frightened, so we continued to shout *mansei*, even inside the room. We just acted giddy with excitement!

Our parents, of course, became very, very concerned. Here we were, girls—*girls*—in prison, and sleeping there overnight. So our parents, almost all of them, brought clothes for us to stay overnight decently. The police kept us there for two full days. They fed us, and every family brought extra food, fearing that we would not be fed. With so many of us, I guess the authorities were relieved to get help feeding us. They treated it like a house arrest.

The police made us write a statement saying we would never do it again, and all of us had to sign it. Then they released us. They did not torture us at all and we had no aftereffects. I think they figured that by staying two nights on the cold floor, we had been punished enough.

It was exciting! What made it so exciting was that our parents thought it was a big thing, a crisis, and we got so much attention from them. Plus we were having fun. Later I found out that the Wŏnsan area had a strong communist underground, of course anti-Japanese, and it was they who had instigated our demonstration.

Boy, I haven't talked about that in a long time!

Another important thing happened near the end of my year in the

Wŏnsan school. The principal, Miss Lucy, a missionary from Canada, made arrangements to send me to Canada to study piano. She finished all the paperwork. All I had to do was graduate and get ready to go.

I MEET A VERY UNCOUTH YOUNG MAN

One day, a young man came to our Vacation Bible School and gave a talk about Korean history. When I went home, I said, "Some young man came to school today. He teaches history pretty well, but he looked ridiculous in straw shoes and baggy peasant pants made of hemp." I had never seen that kind of person, so at home I unabashedly put him down. I said nothing good about him.

When my father, the pastor, heard me, he just smiled. He said he had met this young man in his church in Hwangju and already thought this fellow would make a good husband for me. In those days, not too many girls attended high school, and because I could sing and play the piano, I guess I was considered a good catch. My father really liked this progressive young man, but I said, "How can I have such an uncouth man for a husband?" At that age, a young girl looks for a husband who is handsome and has style, and this fellow was exactly the opposite. Reluctant? I hated the whole idea! I wasn't ready for marriage. I had my own plans—I was going to Canada—but my father pushed this marriage through. He ordered me. In those days, you didn't dare disobey your father.

So in the spring of 1928, the young man, Mr. Kim, and I got engaged. My mother objected, saying, Why should my daughter, who has this great education, get married and end up back in a small rural village near Hwangju? Her education will be wasted.

In response to my mother, father said that my fiancé wasn't going back to the rural area. He qualified for a great job, since he was graduating from a public college. I guess my fate is just not good, because although he was considered a very promising young man, he was arrested by the police!

THE YOUNG MAN BECOMES FAMOUS

At this point, Ms. Yi's story entwines with that of her fiancé, Kim Chando. His family was well-to-do and Christian, and he attended private mission schools.

In 1926 he entered Suwŏn College of Agriculture. He insisted on taking part in the movement to promote education and awareness among farmers. (See chapter 5, page 54.) *At first, his traditional parents did not approve, and even threatened to cut off his tuition, but eventually they relented, and he got his way.*

That young man, Kim Chando, became famous while still in college. In his senior year, 1928, the students said they wanted to show farmers how to improve production. Actually what they did was educate them. They worked side by side in the fields, those students and farmers, and all day the students talked to the farmers, teaching them.

The students taught history, agriculture, and anti-Japanese ideas. For example, they said that without the Japanese exploitation, you farmers would be much better off. You work like dogs all day, break your backs, and the Japanese take most of what you make back to Japan. There is nothing left for you to feed your family.

In winter, in the evenings, the students kept teaching. They went to the outskirts of Suwŏn and taught the adults—mostly farmers from outlying areas. These farmers were totally uneducated, and the young teachers must have looked very educated to them.

Here is one incident that shows that these teachers made an impression. Later, during the Korean War, one young farmer who had been taught by my husband was running away from the communists. His wife gave birth to a baby on the road. In the haste to name the baby, the first name that occurred to the man was my husband's name, so they named the baby Chando. Thus, twenty years later, my husband had a namesake. This name has a double meaning, because the "do" also means "road" and the baby literally was born on the road.

Well, in the autumn of 1928, when the students were doing this teaching on the side, somebody wrote a letter and that letter got into the hands of the police. The police waited for the students to come back to school from the farms and arrested them all at once in the dormitories.

PRISON

In jail, my future husband suffered lots of beatings—very severe. The other students were tortured, too, because they passed the blame around, but my husband freely owned up to being the main plotter. He said he was beaten less than the others, because he answered everything honestly. Some tried to deny that they had ever been out to the farms. They were tortured even more.

Because he was the chief plotter, they put him by himself in an isolation cell. He said the hardest part was having nobody to talk to, all day and all night. The others at least could talk to each other.

Here's how malicious the police were. In winter they moved him to a cell that faced north and exposed him to the freezing northern wind. The cold bit into him, day and night. In summer they put him in a cell facing west, so the afternoon sun blazed in and heated up his room so that he could barely breathe. He said those two, the extreme cold in winter and suffocating heat in summer, were worse than the beatings.

The rules allowed him to have religious books. Because both our families were believers, at the time of our engagement we gave him a Bible, and he took it with him to prison. When he came out of jail, it was worn through, really dog-eared. He knew it inside out.

All the rest of his life he had a skin condition, an itching all over his body—he had it until the day he died. No medicine helped him at all. He acquired it from one of those cells. Once in a while he had a spasm, as though in great shock.

I could not visit him while he was in prison. I knew I was engaged to him, but I didn't want to be engaged to him in the first place. So in my head I said, All right, that's the man to whom I'm engaged, but I didn't know him at all, I had no affection for him. The older generation considered his imprisonment to be a very grave crisis, but as far as I was concerned, I felt, so what? I didn't care. Besides, I really wanted to continue my studies in Canada after I finished high school. That's what I wanted to do—not get married.

I graduated in March 1930, and got a job teaching at another private school. They hired me, I think, because of my singing and piano playing. My younger siblings all told me they became musicians because of me, and my younger brother, Yi Inbŏm, became a famous tenor in the 1950s.

It so happened that Mr. Kim was released from prison shortly after my graduation in March, just one month before I could leave for Canada. I said to myself, Why couldn't he stay in prison just a little longer?

Of the eleven young men arrested, ten were allowed to return to school, but Mr. Kim was in prison so long he missed graduation. He never got a diploma. After the Japanese left, in 1945, the school officials gave him an honorary diploma, seventeen years late.

The police gave Mr. Kim three years' probation with the condition that he not leave his hometown of Hwangju. But they made one exception. They gave him special permission to come to Wŏnsan for our wedding, but even then, a police detective came with him. To the wedding, the police came!

Because of the probation, right after the ceremony we moved back to his home in Hwangju. Since he had to stay there, he started an orchard— remember, he had almost graduated from agricultural college. The police watched his every move, every day, so he could not do any anti-Japanese thing at all.

Unannounced, police came and searched our house for any possible anti-Japanese documents. That really upset me. We never knew when they would appear. Of course we had many books, since we both had been students. Detectives would go into the attic where we stored the books, or the storage room, and search every single book to see if it carried any hint of anti-Japanese content. They came with a huge burlap bag, and any books that they considered suspicious they loaded into their bag. Innocent books! They made all sorts of excuses and carried them away. I got so upset that I threw other books at them, and yelled, "Here, take these, take them all!"

They came so often, we actually got to know them. Because we were a prominent family in the community, when we ran into these detectives in town, they acted very courteous, bowed to us, and exchanged greetings. Then—then they came to our house and tore it apart looking for things that weren't there.

MY DUTIES AS DAUGHTER-IN-LAW

For three years we lived in this rural setting and I served as the traditional daughter-in-law. I had to wait on my parents-in-law, also my sister-in-law who was of marriageable age, also three younger children.

I did attend church and sing in the choir. That was a bit of an outlet, but my duties as daughter-in-law were so overwhelming that I really didn't get involved in church activities. Our household was huge, and I was supposed to run it all. As a prominent family, well-to-do, we had lots of hired help who all needed to be supervised. In the early morning, when these people got ready to go out to the field to work, I had to get up earlier to make lunches for all of them.

I had to be responsible for the household maintenance and supervise the maids, but you can see that I had no preparation for this. I was not trained at all in this way, so I suffered, believe me. On top of that, my parents-in-law were not educated people, so they kept all the old-fashioned ways and did not even want to understand modern ideas. I, on the other hand, had lived in big cities—Wŏnsan, P'yŏngyang—and had almost gone to Canada to study piano. Now, instead, I became only a daughter-in-law.

My own mother's heart ached with great pain over my predicament. I was her only daughter—her treasure. Sometimes she shed tears for me, watching me go backward from modern to traditional.

Even my father, well known nationally in the Presbyterian clergy, tried to come to my aid, but what could he do? So for those three years, I had to endure.

MANCHURIA—APRIL 1933

As soon as my husband's probation was over in March 1933 and all restrictions were removed, my father arranged for the two of us and our infant son to get out of the country and take a teaching post in Manchuria. The job had to be outside Korea, because as a former convict my husband could not get a job anywhere in Korea. The police put a red line across my husband's record, showing that this person was not fit to get a job—he had something bad in his past. So my father arranged the job across the border in Manchuria. He did this for two reasons—the red line, and to get me away from my old-fashioned mother-in-law.

The train stopped before crossing the bridge into Manchuria, and the border police took our permits and arrested my husband. The train left without us. Hours later he came out, beaten, but with the permits. A passerby took us to a spot along the riverbank where people got to Manchuria by walking across the frozen Yalu River. A path stretched ahead of us, beaten down through the snow, exposing the slippery, treacherous ice. Lights blinking on the far shore guided us. I had on cotton socks, my feet were bitter cold, but somehow they did not freeze. I was terrified that the ice would crack beneath us.

Once across the ice into Manchukuo (the Japanese puppet state of Manchuria) we moved to Yangjŏng, a town near Yŏngbyŏn, that had a huge Korean community. We both worked with the Canadian mission. My husband taught biology and chemistry in Ungjin High School. I taught in a kindergarten operated by the church, all part of the mission.

When we arrived, to our amazement, the staff thought that we were the greatest thing that ever happened to them. They asked us to do this, do that, and they put us to work on everything imaginable.

Our son was now one year old, and then we had a daughter. Because of the baby, I had a stroller, a gift from my parents, and whenever I went out, that stroller caused such a commotion that people followed us out of curiosity. A group always surrounded us, gawking at the stroller.

Manchukuo had been under Japanese rule for two years and had a huge army stationed there, but we lived and worked in a Canadian compound, and at that time the Japanese didn't interfere. Later, of course, even the missionaries could not be protected. They were arrested and put in prison. But at the time we were there, things were still quiet.

My husband did not do any specific anti-Japanese activities, but in his classrooms he told students about Korea and instilled in them anti-Japanese sentiments. To this day, we receive letters from former students who say they remember what he told them about Japanese exploitation and the need for independence. Many teachers did the same thing.

WE RETURN TO KOREA

Five years later, in 1938, for several reasons, we moved back to Korea. The winters in Manchuria were so cold that it was not fit to live there, the war had started in Manchuria, and my husband's parents simply told us to return. We could not disobey parents, so we returned to Hwangju.

When we returned, the police resumed their constant surveillance of us. They watched my husband every minute. When my son attended primary school, his classmates whispered among themselves, "His father is a convict, he was in jail," so our son got into fights with those boys.

Our family survived. We survived the Japanese, and we survived the communists. But looking back, two things really sadden me, even today. First, that constant harassment of my husband by the Japanese—very stressful.

Second, seeing my own father, the minister, come out of jail with his body all black and blue. Instead of being concerned about my father's well being, the congregation launched into hallelujahs and songs of praise. I still don't understand that reasoning. How can those people rejoice? It's hard for a daughter. Even my mother praised the Lord. Nobody cried. Nobody shed tears. And they jailed him many times.

The Sermon on the Mount says rejoice when you suffer in God's name. It must be that. But I didn't like my father suffering. When he was released, and came out with tattered clothes, barely walking, it just broke my heart.

EPILOGUE, 1945–1995

From 1945 to 1950 both Mr. and Mrs. Kim were active in politics. Mrs. Kim became a delegate from their hometown to the newly organized provisional government in P'yŏngyang, and "she even cut her hair." Because of her influence, her daughter majored in politics (at a men's college, Korea University), and later her granddaughter also majored in politics. Mr. Kim's second daughter married a man who later became the Korean Ambassador to Poland.

In 1947 Mr. Kim fled the communists by going south alone, and his wife and children followed later, dressed as peasants to escape detection. In South Korea, he was again put in prison, this time suspected of being a North Korean spy. His son advocated for him and, upon his release, cared for his wounds from the prison beatings.

Later, Mr. Kim got a government job as head of the Agricultural Technological Institute in Suwŏn, and Mrs. Kim taught music in middle school and high school.

Mr. Kim's younger brother was indeed a communist and stayed in North Korea. Mrs. Kim's younger brother, a famous pianist, left his wife and children in the south and went back to the north where he married again, had another family, and eventually died. This man's South Korean daughter (Mrs. Kim's niece) went north in the early 1990s, located all her half-siblings, and found that they all had become musicians and artists, another family tradition. She joined her half-brother, and they played a piano concert on stage and on television for Kim Il Sŏng's (president of North Korea, 1948–1994) birthday.

Mr. Kim dearly wanted to return to see northern Korea, but said he would never go through the "back door"; he would wait until he could go with dignity through the front door from Seoul. He never got the chance.

In 1990, living in San Francisco, Mr. Kim received a commendation from the Korean government for anti-Japanese activity and suffering. He died of illness in San Francisco in 1994, and Mrs. Kim died in 1996 after being hit by a car.

Kim Wŏnkuk (right) and classmate, August 1937, third year Kilju Agriculture High School, North Hamgyŏng Province. (Courtesy of Kim Wŏnkuk. Photo restored by Colleen Redpath)

PART TWO

Change by Coercion

OVERVIEW

The years of assimilation arrived, as the Japanese levied onto Koreans increasing constraints, obligations, and eventually conscription. The changes began in 1931 when Japan turned Manchuria into Manchukuo, and escalated as Japan moved against China in 1937 and on into the Second World War.

The Governor-General talked of this period as the period of "constructive change" enhanced by new government agencies ushering in tighter political, economic, and thought control. The High Police (often called the "secret" or "thought" police) were a special section of the police whose very name held terror for most people. The power of personal choice slid into the background as citizens dealt with a dizzying array of pressures forcing them to speak Japanese, honor the Japanese Emperor, and even change their names to Japanese. By 1940, the entire population was organized into Neighborhood Associations of ten-family units in order to monitor compliance with all official instructions.

The following chapters focus on Koreans whose lives changed significantly owing to these constraints. Mr. Lee tells of his years in the Japanese prison system, Miss Yu recalls the long arm of the "thought police" monitoring her family's every move far away in Shanghai, and Mr. Chŏng tells of his work in a Japanese shipyard during the last years of the war. Between these chapters are the vignettes of others who lived their lives under the duress of daily imposed obligations.

8 : A Red Line Marks My Record

YI HAJŎN [LEE HA JUN]

Student (m) b. 1921, South P'yŏngan Province

After graduation from high school in 1940, I went to Hosei University in Tokyo, Japan. In less than a year, the police department from my home in P'yŏngyang dispatched five secret police detectives all the way to Tokyo to arrest me.

Because of that arrest, I now own two documents that verify the red line across my record—my indictment from the Japanese police that sent me to prison, and a commendation from the Korean government for the same set of circumstances. Of ten such acknowledged activists who have moved to the San Francisco area, I am one of the few still alive to tell the story—which for me, begins among the honored and wealthy families of P'yŏngyang.

On my father's side, Grandfather was a government official under the Chosŏn dynasty, and a rather prominent person in P'yŏngyang. One of his sons by a concubine opened the very first auto dealership in that city. On my mother's side, Grandfather was one of the richest people in all P'yŏngyang, but my father's generation squandered all the money.

Father graduated from Meiji University in Japan—very rare for a Korean in those days. He became principal of a Korean high school, Kwangsŏng High School. I remember him being put in prison several times, going in and coming out, but I never knew the reason.

COMMERCIAL HIGH SCHOOL

I started attending Sung'in Business High School in P'yŏngyang in 1936, when I was fifteen. This private Christian school had been established by

Mr. Cho Mansik, an ardent nationalist active in the Independence Movement. We had a Korean principal, Kim Hangsik. The school fostered a sense of Korean identity, quite different from public [Japanese-run] schools.

During an hour of chapel every day, inspirational speakers told us about Korea's proud past and our present predicament. Speakers included such famous people as Ham Sŏkhŏn[1] and Cho Mansik himself. Mr. Cho almost became president of the whole of Korea right after the Japanese left, and he served in the first committee to run the Soviet half of Korea when it divided, but eventually he was jailed by Kim Il Sŏng's group because he would not go along with their plans.

It was during my third year in high school that a respected and prominent independence activist, Mr. Ahn Ch'angho,[2] passed away. The news changed the direction of my life.

I remember the date clearly—March 10. I passed by the office of a Korean newspaper called *Dong-a Ilbo,* glanced up, and read on the bulletin board in huge letters, "Mr. Ahn Ch'angho dies."

At that time, I had no idea who he was or why his death merited such a prominent announcement, but when I got home, I found Mother crying her heart out. I asked Father what was wrong, and he said she was crying about Mr. Ahn's death. I wondered what kind of person this Mr. Ahn could have been, that even my mother mourned him.

I felt ignorant that I didn't know about him, but, you realize, at high school age, we were still looking for our own identity. Well, I decided to find out about Mr. Ahn, what he did, his life. I asked around—my classmates—my teachers—everybody. I discovered he was a fervent independence activist. A true patriot. And he died for the country as a martyr because he died in prison. So I started reading all the books written by him and about him.

I BECOME A PATRIOT

I completely turned around. I got interested in Korean literature and the writings, for example, of people like Mr. Yi Kwangsu, which had an undercurrent of patriotism, love of country.

Several others determined with me that we could not just sit idly by, going to school, doing nothing. We had to become more active toward our independence. We got together in secret, forming what they called a circle, a group. The members of this group included four from my high school and two from a public high school called Second P'yŏngyang High School (the First High School was Japanese). That made six of us.

We exchanged books, critiqued them, discussed them, analyzed them. We chose books about Korean history and Korean heroes. These were hard to come by in those days, as you can imagine.

We invited Mr. Ham Sŏkhŏn as a speaker to our secret meetings. Everyone admired him as an independent activist and thinker. At the time he was teaching farther north at Osan High School in Chŏngju, another hotbed of resistance. He came all the way from Chŏngju to be with the six of us.

Though we were still young, we knew that we had better keep all this from the police, so we met at my house on the pretext of learning the Bible—Mr. Ham was a Bible authority, but in addition, he explained the predicaments that we Koreans were in at the present time, and said we had to be wide awake, alert, to push things through for the good of Korea. His words impelled us to action, and it was all in the form of a Bible study.

We decided to raise funds for educating people, so we each donated what we could—one yen, two yen, and so forth—a huge amount for students. We also decided to make it look very, very official, so we made club bylaws, a constitution. I served as the male president and we also had a female president, Kim Okgil, who later became president of Ewha University in Seoul. We knew each other well while we were growing up.

We even knew a piece of forbidden information. We heard about a provisional government of Korea in exile in Shanghai. One of my classmates heard it from somebody, and so we all knew about it. We even heard that this government in exile cooperated with Chinese nationalists under Chiang Kai-shek to fight against the Japanese. It surprised us to hear that somewhere, someone actually was fighting the Japanese.

So our group did three things—discussed books, raised funds, and recruited new members. We kept at our activities all during our last two years of high school; then we all graduated and went our separate ways. Three of us went to Tokyo for advanced studies, one went to medical school in P'yŏngyang, others got jobs. Through it all, the group's activities were never far from my mind.

Mr. Ham Sŏkhŏn, who had given us the talk, was thought by the Japanese to be a dangerous activist, and therefore constantly watched. The secret police detectives regularly searched his house. During one of these searches, they discovered a letter from one of the members of our group, telling Mr. Ham about our desire to increase the scope and membership of the group.

Mr. Ham should have thrown that letter away. Maybe he kept it in order to reply. In any event, they found it. So, from there, things started to unravel. They interrogated Mr. Ham, and to make things worse, he had no idea of the true intent of our group, so he told them all he knew. When police asked for names, since he thought it was harmless, he told.

After obtaining the names, the police first got hold of the medical student in P'yŏngyang. This student, under heavy torture and great pain, finally confessed about our purpose, objectives, and activities. When they discovered our plot, they said, "We really have got something here," and they gave it full priority. They dispatched five detectives all the way from P'yŏngyang to Tokyo to arrest the three of us who had gone there to study.

One of the three of us in Tokyo heard a rumor about arrests being made back home in P'yŏngyang, and he took off to Manchuria to join a relative there. He said he would go on to China and join the Korean activists in exile.

The other fellow and I kept on studying, and those detectives just came one day and got us. They bound our arms behind our backs with rope. They took me to Nakano Police Station in Tokyo and I spent a week there. It was a monkey house, there were so many jammed into the cell with me, for all kinds of crimes.

Then they took us all the way back to P'yŏngyang, by train, by ferry, and train again. They put me in a cell at Taedong Police Station and put the other fellow in prison across the river, to separate us.

Whom did I find in the very next cell, but Mr. Ham, himself. He would not tell me why he was in prison, but it is true that he was arrested for his Christian resistance. Once they took him to the torture chamber, and when he came back he could hardly speak or move at all.

I never found out what trumped-up charges brought those men there. You must realize that the prison rule was no talking, so only when the guards moved away could we whisper a bit. That is why we shared so little. You really had to whisper under your breath, otherwise you'd be in even more trouble. They enforced the iron rule to keep quiet, all day, at all times.

Japanese cavalry on patrol near P'yŏngyang, 1904.
(Courtesy of the Library of Congress, LC-USZ62-99655)

On the other hand, they allowed us to read books, including even the Bible. I suspected it was because we were in for a long-term incarceration.

We were arrested in January 1941, and arrived in P'yŏngyang the first of February. Then we waited a whole month before being taken for interrogation.

The secret police detectives came, both Japanese and Korean, and tortures began. The Korean detective became the actual torturer. Also, a Korean clerk wrote down everything. They slapped my face, cheeks. They forced me to drink gallons of water. If you keep drinking, you can't breathe and you faint. They had this down to a science. They knew exactly how many seconds they had to wait until they revived me, or I'd die. Of course I was bound, so I could not move at all. One man pours water down my face and the other stands by with a timer. After I faint, they wait so many seconds and revive me. Then they say, "Do you want that again? Why don't you confess? Tell the truth."

I told them I had no more to tell—that I had already told them everything I knew.

"Are those true accounts?" they asked.

They kept asking me for additional people we tried to recruit. That's what they wanted to know, so they could arrest more people. I kept repeating that I had told them everything—I knew nothing else.

The first day was the longest, really bad. I endured continual slapping, beating, again and again. They kept beating me, black and blue, yelling in my ear, "That was a mistake you made." Nothing broke, but I had bruises and welts all over my body. I think, since I was young, just twenty-one, I recovered more quickly than the older prisoners. But even at my age, those bruises didn't go away for months and months.

They made me sign a confession. Of course I signed—no choice!

Then they passed our files to the prosecutor's office and just left me in my cell for six months, into the summer, waiting for the trial. The weather turned stiflingly hot.

Next, they moved me to the actual prison. It had two sections—one for those already sentenced and serving their terms, and another for those waiting trial. While there, the prosecutor's office summoned us for another investigation. For two days they interrogated us, going over every single article, asking, "Is this true? Is this true? Did you confess to this? And this?" No torture this time, just questions.

I waited in the prison for another six months until finally the trial began. It turned bitterly cold, so it must have become winter again.

At this time I had regular clothes on, not prisoner's garb, because we weren't convicted yet. They actually allowed us to get clothes and some food from our family members who lived nearby. But although our families could bring us food, it had to be purchased from the prison caterer, who had a prescribed menu for prisoners.

I made no friends among the prisoners. A great gulf existed between us. Hearing their stories of why they got arrested, I simply could not identify with them. They were truly the bottom rungs of society. Pickpockets, thieves, murderers. I could not bridge that chasm.

GUILTY AS CHARGED

I know exactly the date we went to trial—December 8, 1941, Pearl Harbor day. It was December 7 in the west, but the eighth already in Asia. Of course, we didn't know at the time that a war had started.

Change by Coercion

In those days, the Japanese were very touchy, watching for any sign of anti-Japanese sentiments or activities, and with very little provocation they would arrest anybody. Often the police beat people up and then released them, just to frighten everybody. But in our case, since what we did really was anti-Japanese, and we had confessed everything, the prosecutor had no choice but to convict us. The court had six *volumes* of specific crimes, and ours fit exactly. It was a classic crime.

In the prosecutor's opening speech, he said, "This is an historic occasion, on the day when we are embarking on a new world war for our empire, we are also prosecuting those who plot to undermine the Japanese empire. It is indeed fitting that these anti-Japanese students be severely punished." Very eloquent. At my expense.

We students stood there before the three judges. We were all there, all six of us, including the one who had fled to Manchuria, for detectives had gone after that one and found him before he even got to China.

The trial lasted from morning to night for two full days. About a week after the trial, they announced the verdict. The system was such that they then gave us a week to decide whether or not to appeal to a higher court. If you chose not to appeal, then you had to sign—put down your signature seal (*tojang*). Of course, they found us all guilty.

The prosecutor's office demanded seven years—*seven*—for each of us, but our defense attorney argued in our behalf, saying, "These are young people. It's a first offense. They won't do it again. Be tolerant." Acknowledging the guilt, but trying to ease the sentence. The actual sentence came down as two and a half years.

For lesser crimes, such as civil cases or thefts, they count the time already spent in prison awaiting trial as part of the sentence. But for us, the sentence began after the trial. So I actually spent three and a half years in prison.

THE RED UNIFORM

On December 26, 1941, I changed my clothes to the red uniform of a convict. I do not forget that date.

The Japanese celebrated the 25 of December as a national holiday commemorating the death of their previous emperor, Taisho. In the west, December 25 is Christmas. For me, it is the day I formally donned the red garb of a convict. First you put on underwear, because it was winter. Even that is red, faded red, after being worn too long and washed too often. It looks like pajamas, but still it is the prisoner's color.

To change my clothes to the convict's uniform, I had to go out into the hallway and wait for my uniform to arrive. To my surprise, I saw the famous Reverend Chu Kich'ŏl. Even I, young as I was, had heard about him. I noticed him, right there, in this same prison with me. I went over to him and shook hands. He grasped my hands and told me, "At your young age, do not waste your energy frivolously. Conduct yourself carefully, so that you can accomplish big things later in life." While he grasped my hands, he prayed over me. It made a great impression on me—an historic moment for me. Later, after I was discharged, I learned that he had died in prison. Many martyrs died in prison while languishing under the harsh conditions, waiting for their trial, and being tortured every day. None of them were actually convicted. On paper, the Japanese constitution guaranteed freedom of religion.

They crammed about ten prisoners into one cell. I was the only political prisoner—the others were simply general criminals, all Korean except for one Japanese. The Japanese prisoner said he was in for some economic crime, but my cell-mates whispered that he was a planted spy, and we should be very, very careful of him. I didn't have to worry, because as a political prisoner, I soon got transferred out of that group and into a solitary cell.

An unusually severe winter arrived that year, even for northern Korea. Rumors said that even the cows outside froze to death. The guard issued me a tatami mat, one pair of socks, one cotton-filled set of underwear, and the red uniform. That was it. The severe cold caused my ears to get frostbitten and my breath to freeze on the windowpane. The guards gave me one cup of water a day, and if I didn't drink it fast enough, it turned to ice right there in the cup. I must say, I almost died that first month.

There wasn't much rice for our meals, so they mixed it with wheat, barley, beans, anything to extend it. They used ten different-sized containers of rice. A prisoner got the larger amount if he engaged in physical labor, and the smallest portion if he sat all day and didn't work at all. When I first entered prison, they handed me a number eight portion, about one fistful of rice, three times a day. Along with that came a little bowl of boiled salt water. Once in a while, a piece of vegetable floated in it, or one or two pieces of *kimchi* (pickled cabbage). That's all. Once in a great while, they

Change by Coercion

gave us a piece of rotten fish, all marinated, but rotten. Sometimes only the fish's tail.

AT WORK IN THE FACTORY

I worked during the day in a cosmetics factory within the prison walls, some distance from our cells. A civilian company contracted with the prison to set up the factory and use convicts as workers. They made face cream, soap, and other cosmetics, working from eight in the morning until about five in the afternoon, with no rest except for the lunch break.

Listen to this. They forced us to take off all our clothes, all of them, and run stark naked from our cells to the entrance of that factory. There, we put on factory uniforms and worked all day. At the end of work, we reversed the process. Guards lined up all along the route to watch us. No matter how cold. No matter what. We ran naked, they said, for security reasons.

They did let us bathe about once a week. We had a huge shower room, and we all showered together. As you can see, with hundreds of convicts, many with varying degrees of infections, most people got diseases and skin rashes and other things. They gave us some medicines to apply to our skin, but it didn't help much.

Once a month they allowed us to receive visitors for fifteen minutes each, but visitors could bring nothing in from the outside except books. And they inspected what kind of books. The Bible passed inspection before the Second World War started, but after that, even the Bible was not allowed. Buddhist scriptures, however, they did allow, so I studied a great deal about Buddhism. I really concentrated. To this day, I know a lot about the Buddhists and their doctrines. Once a week they herded us into the auditorium and a Buddhist monk came and held services, full of their chanting. To the Japanese, Buddhism is so like Shinto, the distinction is so blurred, that they think it is almost the same.

MOVED AGAIN

After another six months, the prison authorities moved me again, this time to a prison far south of Seoul, in Kongju, South Ch'ungch'ŏng Province. The majority of these political prisoners were leftist activists. The nonradical nationalists like us were very few. Those leftist agitators remained in their cells the entire time. Among them was the already well known Chu Yŏngha, who went to North Korea after liberation from the Japanese and there became important. Several other well-known partisan prisoners also spent years there in prison with us.

Besides the political prisoners, the Kongju prison held criminals from all over the country who had had nervous breakdowns or had abnormal minds. These mentally ill prisoners lived in a separate ward, but they were there in the same prison with us.

One thing I must say. Though we were in prison and physically confined, they did not do psychological brainwashing, mental torture, or force us to do Shinto shrine worship. We were just physically confined. Perhaps because we were political prisoners, and well educated, the prison guards actually treated us with respect. Our education was superior to theirs, and our crime was simply having a different ideology, not crimes against society, so they did treat us differently, gentlemanly.

Put on kitchen duty, I found I could get more food, and get the first choice of food. It may have been poor rice, or rice mixed with other things, but whatever it was, I could eat my fill. However, there was almost no nourishment value in any of the food, so I continued to weaken.

The war raged in full swing and rationing had begun, so some of our food came down from Manchuria and it was horrid. In Manchuria, beans were squeezed for their oil. After the oils were squeezed out, the residue was sent to the prisons and mixed with various grains for our food. We saw almost no rice, ever. This garbage mixture served as our staple. It was really bad stuff. It went right through our bodies, leaving no nourishment.

The other bad thing was that mold formed very readily on this stuff. When we cooked it, it always gave off a strange odor. After I ate too much of that, I suffered terrible sickness. Other people, the weak and the elderly, died after eating this.

One day, the Emperor's birthday, the butcher slaughtered a pig to be fed to the prisoners. But first, pieces were sent to officials in the prison, and then to officials in the town. We have an old saying, "When the cow is slaughtered, you only get to smell the soup," meaning, everybody else got some, and by the time our turn came, nothing was left. So in our own soup, if we saw even a drop or two of oil floating on the surface, we said, "Yah, this is good."

Well, that day, in the soup, we had a lot of oil drops from that pig. Being on the kitchen detail, I got to drink all I wanted, so of course, I drank too much. The next day I had intense diarrhea. My body was just too weak to fight it off.

Again in 1944, I got the same ailment. I was terribly sick. I couldn't eat, and I had persistent diarrhea. In fact, I was still sick on the day I was released.

Another thing I had all through prison was boils. I had three or four episodes like that in prison, where I almost died. But obviously, I recovered. I believe I survived because I was young and healthy when I went in. Many, many old people died.

I served every day of the two and a half years of my sentence. There was no early release.

RELEASE — SUMMER 1944

As soon as I got out I went back to P'yŏngyang, and lived quietly. I did not want to attract any attention at all. Many of my relatives were doctors, and they gave me medicine until finally I got well and the diarrhea stopped.

One section in the secret police had the job of keeping released prisoners under surveillance. They visited me regularly and watched all my comings and goings. They came at any time, unannounced. They called out, "Hi there, how are you doing?"

They tried to convince me to change my thoughts and ideas. They also urged me to get married, telling me it would help me settle down and make their job easier. But, listen to this, what parents would let their daughter marry *me*, a convict, with a red line on my record? In those days, being a prisoner meant that the rest of my life was dead. Nobody wanted to have a thing to do with me.

VISIT FROM THE FAMOUS PATRIOT, CHO MANSIK

Mr. Cho Mansik had founded that Christian high school from which I graduated, and I was the only graduate of that school who was arrested and served time in prison. That's how he knew of me. He visited me to celebrate my release from prison and brought with him two large pieces of beef. In those days, beef was almost impossible to obtain. This gift amazed me. A *huge* present. Meat was so rare.

He grasped my hand, congratulated me, and said how thankful he was that I had come out alive. I really appreciated his visit. If the police had found out that we two met, who knows what charges they might have trumped up against us both.

I needed to work, to regain my health, my strength. Because I was a criminal, I could not be a soldier even if I wanted to be, but they could still draft me for factory work. To avoid that work draft, I had to get a job they considered essential.

I went off to live with my sister in Sariwŏn city and I got a job with an ox-cart freight company. Although I had an office job, and it was only an ox cart company, the job still was related to transportation and that made me exempt even from the work-draft. I supervised the loading and unloading of materials from the carts.

I noticed Japanese refugees streaming down from Manchuria through Korea headed for the Japanese mainland, and from them I head rumors that Japan might surrender. We didn't know it, but Russia had gotten into the war in the north, and these Japanese were fleeing while they could. I returned to P'yŏngyang.

EPILOGUE, 1945–1995

After liberation from Japanese rule in 1945, Mr. Yi received a letter from the North Korean communists, the People's Reconstruction Committee of P'yŏngyang, saying, "Mr. Yi, let us work together to build our fatherland." The day after he got the letter, he packed his things and traveled on foot to South Korea to get away from the communists.

His family also moved to the south, and his father became a high school principal again. But during the Korean War, the communists came down, occupied their city, and killed his father, just because he was a high school principal.

The president of Yŏnhŭi University (now Yŏnsei University) urged Mr. Yi to get more education, and he moved to America to attend the University of California, Berkeley. Next came a job at the Monterey Language School in California, training soldiers to learn Korean for their work in the Korean War. Monterey remained his home until he retired, and he and his wife live there still. Mr. Yi served as president of the Association for Korean Independence, a movement active in the 1920s and 1930s and continuing to this day in northern California, honoring those who were active in the Independence Movement.

9 : Passive Resistance

By the late 1930s, overt resistance continued only along Korea's northern border. The Righteous Armies and freedom fighters of the early years faded from view, and even the peasant protests of the 1920s and early '30s disappeared due to the increase in repressive police power and efficient communication networks. People turned to passive, everyday forms of resistance—hiding crops, feigning ignorance, conveniently disappearing—or protested in ways only slightly more obvious, singing songs with hidden meanings, taking part in labor strikes, spreading anti Japanese rumors, and, especially Christians, refusing to bow to Shinto shrines.[1]

Barrington Moore, when writing about the German workers of 1848, could just as well have been talking about the Koreans: "Misery there certainly was, and in new and disturbing forms as well as old and familiar ones. But the main fact is simply this: the overwhelming majority of those whose 'objective' situation would qualify them as being somehow the victims of injustice took no active part in the events of the period. As far as it is possible to tell now, they just sat tight, tried to make do in their daily lives, and waited for the outcome."[2]

YANG SŎNGDŎK,
(m) b. 1919, electrical engineer, South Ch'ungch'ŏng Province:
My hometown of Kanggyŏng was an important seaport. It is at the mouth of the Kŭm River, the site of the old Paekche capital, where for centuries much trade took place with China and Japan. My grandfather was a rice dealer, and in those days all the rice harvest was brought to this seaport

Oldest Shinto shrine in Korea, on a hilltop overlooking Pusan,
showing the torii gate and steps leading to the shrine at the top, circa 1925.
(Norman Thorpe Collection)

and then shipped to Japan. Because of the town's importance, many, many Japanese lived there.

I remember that when I was in fourth or fifth grade (1929–30) the Japanese forbade Koreans to wear their traditional white clothing, but they couldn't enforce the ban. Those Japanese set up huge tubs of water—dirty, dark water—at street corners everywhere. Whenever they saw people in white clothes passing by, they sprayed them with this dark water.

We kids sometimes played practical jokes on our Japanese neighbors. We crept out in the middle of night and dug holes outside their houses' front entrance. We filled the holes with night soil [human excrement] from the outhouse and then covered it up with clean soil. The next morning they stepped in it!

Sometimes we threw chicken droppings onto their laundry hung out to dry. That wasn't so bad. We did these things when we were in primary school. As I look back now, they certainly weren't good things to do, but we were boys and we egged each other on.

As I grew older, I found more acceptable ways to voice resistance. One thing we used was music. I first heard the song *"Pongsŏnhwa"* when I was

Change by Coercion

in technical high school. It speaks of a flower springing up to new life. The Japanese knew we sang it as an independence song, and later, after we all learned it, they banned it.

KIM SŎBUN, (f) b. 1914, housewife, South Kyŏngsang Province:
My cousins tried to bring down the Japanese government by secretly recruiting communist activists to establish a communist government. To stay alive, they never stayed in one place.

I remember one cousin who walked so silently I could not hear him at all. Once when he came to our house, I looked at the soles of his shoes. They were a special soft material that killed the sound. I was terrified whenever they came to visit us, for fear we would be arrested, but my husband didn't seem to mind.

I also knew—knew *about*—a young woman who was really active. In my first semester of high school, 1930, the Kwangju student uprising had just started and Japanese police came all through our dorm, hunting for plotters. To my surprise, they arrested one of the girls right down the hall from me as a ringleader.

Later my father purchased a small house in Pusan so I could live there and commute to school. In those days we didn't have running water, so we went to a central well for water. One time, getting water, there was that same girl! I was so happy to see her, but she clearly did not want to talk to me—she pretended not to see me.

One day the whole Japanese police force swooped down on our neighborhood, doing a house-to-house search. I saw them arrest this girl again, along with some others. I felt bad for her. She was only two grades above me.

I don't know what fate bound us together, but years later, when my husband was transferred to Hadong city in South Kyŏngsang Province, one day someone came in to ask a favor of him, and it turned out to be this very woman with her husband. When I first saw her, I was so stunned that my heart sank to my stomach. I wasn't sure whether to welcome her with open arms or to be wary. She must have been arrested, released, and gotten married. The two of them must have been strong activists.

Christians gained the reputation of being anti-Japanese, partly because some groups refused to bow to the Japanese Emperor or the gods of Shinto. The local Neighborhood Association leaders watched those who attended church and then

harassed them, persuading them not to attend—sometimes with words, and some-
times by withholding rations cards, prison, or death.

SIN KWANGSŎNG, (m) b. 1915, farmer, North Kyŏngsang Province:
I grew up on a farm so poor we didn't even have electricity. My father
was one of the first converts to the Presbyterian church in my home village.
In the early days, we had no problems, but when the war came, persecu-
tions came. The Japanese got more and more strict, and bothered us at
every turn.

Our church started out with about forty adults, but every day, with all
the pestering, members stopped coming. A few women continued, but
soon I became the only young man. Even my brothers stopped coming.

We didn't have a pastor, so I took charge. Well, no one else would do
it. I studied the Bible a bit and then led the service. After my one-minute
sermon, we mostly sang hymns and read the Bible. We had only Sunday
worship—no Wednesday evening and no early morning prayer time.

We had to wait until the Japanese police detective arrived to begin the
service. He always sat down right in the front row. He never closed our
church, but he was always there, listening, watching.

We had other problems, too. My elder brother, for example, went to a
Bible school before there were seminaries. The police knew when he left
and when he came back. They came around all the time to ask what he did,
what he studied, and he had to report every one of his activities. The police
treated him as if he was on parole, having to tell them his every move. After
a while it just got to be too much to deal with, and he stopped going to
that school.

My only dealings with the police were because we were members of the
Christian Church. There was no other reason for them to bother with me,
because I paid my taxes and I obeyed their laws.

PAK CHUN'GI, (f) b. 1914, housewife, Kyŏnggi Province:
My first contact with Christianity came in 1930 when I was sixteen. An
American missionary stood under a tree and preached the gospel. His fluent Korean surprised me, and I listened out of curiosity. I felt I should become Christian, but once I got home, I forgot about it.

After I had my first two children, and behind my husband's back, I went to church—Sin Gwang Methodist Church. When I first started attending, about 1936, we met in secret in someone's living room.

The service lasted about an hour. When we sang hymns, we sang in our minds, we didn't sing out loud at all. No fellowship. Just the service, for fear of being discovered. We never met on Sunday because it would be too obvious. We met on Wednesday evening.

The Japanese police would arrest us if they found out, because instead of worshipping at the Shinto shrine, we were believing in Christianity. Many people that I knew were arrested.

Mostly the group was women, with very few men. All of us were young, except for the preacher, a woman in her fifties. She would secretly preach the gospel and do evangelism work in the neighborhood. I owe it to her for my becoming Christian.

Nobody knew that I went there. After the war, when it was safe, it came to light. We decided to build a house, and we bought the lot and tore down the old shack. I thought it would be good to have a prayer of dedication for the new house, so I invited Pastor Hong from the newly established church. He came and gave the prayer, and that is when my husband found out. Although he would never attend services, he decided that the church taught good things, so he told all our children to attend church with me.

The injustices in the next three stories left lasting scars in the memories of the men involved.

U CH'AN'GU,
(m) b. 1916, railway worker, North Ch'ungch'ŏng Province:
About 1936 we had a young student working for us. There was a long whip in our office, and whenever this student made some slight mistake, the Japanese superiors made him stand still and they hit him with this whip, right on his forehead. I can still see him, standing there, tears running down his face. Even then I thought, why does he have to put up with this persecution?

CHŎNG T'AE'IK, (m) b. 1911, farmer, Kangwŏn Province:
Twice a year, a group went around inspecting the cleanliness of each house. People had to have their houses very, very clean. Somehow, they al-

ways made me the head of the local neighborhood cell, so I became responsible for seeing that all the houses in my group were clean.

As head of my cell, I had to tag along with the Japanese inspector. We looked not only at the house, but also the thatched-roof shed for the animals.

Well, when crops weren't good, farmers couldn't afford to replace the straw in the roofs. At one house, the thatch had not been replaced and it had rotted. We got in there, with a ceiling so low you could touch it. The inspector poked it with his prod, and since it was rotten, it all came down. Of course there were bugs in that roof, and it all fell to the floor—the rotten straw and the worms.

The inspector screamed at the owner of the house and made him, forced him, to eat the worms! I was sick. I wanted to stop him but I didn't dare say a thing. It was so insulting—humiliating—cruel. He could have fined him! But right there, he forced him to eat the worms. That is the bitterest memory I have of the colonial rule.

CHŎNG KŬMJAE [CHUNG KUM JAE],
(m) b. 1919, day laborer, North Ch'ungch'ŏng Province:
I think you never heard a story like mine! I fought with a police chief— *chief!*—and lived to tell about it.

I grew up in a farm village and finished grade four in school—that's enough, my father said. Then I worked on the farm. When I was sixteen, about 1935, I decided this really was a dead-end job, so I left home and went up to Seoul.

I got work as a day laborer, going every day to the station outside East Gate. After about four months the whole group of us moved to Hwanghae Province to lay the second railroad track from Seoul to the Manchuria border.

Up there one day, a man stopped me and asked me to work in his restaurant. He wanted me to feed the pigs and cows, but more important, he wanted me to go collecting all the money people owed him. He said his customers, people from the post office and police station, usually paid their bills once a month instead of paying when they ate. Then sometimes they didn't pay at all. The owner thought a younger fellow might get away with being more pushy and make the officers pay up sooner.

I took his job—it was easier than railroad work—and stayed with him for two years. Then one day, disaster!

Change by Coercion

You know, a restaurant keeps lots of meat and other foods. Well, a cat kept stealing from us, and the owner told another young man and me to get rid of that cat. In the middle of the night we put meat out in a trap. We caught the cat and killed it. All in secret—nobody knew—problem solved.

The next morning I went out as usual to feed the pigs in the backyard, when the local police chief came up to the fence and said, "Come here."

He took me to the police station, into his own office, and asked, "Did you kill a cat last night?"

So he already knew, of course, that I did it. I had to own up and say, "Yes, sir." Remember, I was only twenty years old and facing the chief of police.

"Do you know that it was *my* favorite cat? Since you killed my cat, I am going to kill you."

He told me to kneel down on the floor with my head hanging down. He went to his wall, took down a samurai sword, and came back to me. With both hands, he raised that sword high above his head.

He really meant to kill me! Right there! He could get away with anything, anything at all, especially with a lowly errand boy. He could make up any excuse.

I glanced up, saw the sword above my head, and panicked! I leapt up. My foot shot out. I kicked his groin. Of course, he didn't expect anything at all, so he fell over backward, all curled up. I kicked at him again and again, blindly. I struck at his head, his eyeballs.

Then suddenly, shaking with fear, I realized I was in big trouble! I fled outside. As I ran, I tried to think. Don't go back to the restaurant. Run into the mountains. I decided to flee to P'yŏngyang city, thinking it should be easy to hide there in the crowds.

I worked my way through the wilderness, mountain by mountain, far from the highway. It took me four days to get to the city. As I entered P'yŏngyang, a policeman stopped me on a routine check. He asked me where my hometown was and what I was doing now. I said I was on my way to visit an elder brother. He looked me up and down and said to empty my pockets so he could see what I had with me.

I had this and that, but I also had my savings book of twenty-seven yen, a reasonably large amount. When he saw that much money saved, he said, "That's good enough. You may go." If he had taken me to jail, I would have been finished—every police station was on the alert to catch me.

In those days, the easiest place to hide was among day laborers, so I went back into the labor gang, laying another rail track. I kept that up for several years, and sent money home to my family without putting down my address. That way, they knew I was safe but hiding somewhere. The police went to my family in North Ch'ungch'ŏng Province looking for me to arrest me, but since my family really didn't know where I was, finally the police just gave up.

When it was safe, I went home. I had to take over the farm because I became eldest son when my brother died. I learned then that I had blinded that police chief and he had been sent back to Japan.

Look at me! Even today—thinking of it, talking of it—my body trembles at the memory.

Change by Coercion

10 : Thought Police Stay for Dinner

YU HYEGYŎNG

Housewife (f) b. 1924, Manchuria

One thing I like to brag about is that Father invented a mint pill called *Indan*, like a peppermint, that is good for many things, and he had it patented in China. He sold these mints. Father was a practicing physician in Korea, but moved us to Manchuria (where I was born in 1924) and then to Shanghai, looking for a better life. He found a better job, teaching physics and chemistry at three Chinese colleges in Shanghai, but he did not escape the watchful eye of the Japanese thought police.

I was sent to a Japanese primary school in the Japanese section of Shanghai. I don't recall a single incident of being mistreated by the Japanese. I went on to a Japanese high school, also. Only one or two students in each class were Korean. Altogether, there were only thirteen of us Korean girls going to school in Shanghai, and when we went back to Korea after the end of the war, we formed an alumnae group in Seoul and we met regularly.

Now I will show you the extent of the Japanese police presence, even in Shanghai. To explain, I must tell you more about my father.

He was a professor at the college in Shanghai and a well-known calligrapher, but the Japanese secret police considered him to be a potential conspirator against them. They were especially concerned because with his position and assets, he could provide funds to other Koreans for anti-Japanese activities.

In Shanghai, a provisional Korean government-in-exile published a newspaper called *Independence*, written in the Korean script, *han'gŭl*. It

Ŭnjin School, South Ch'ungch'ŏng Province. Graduation, 1938. The label shows the year in the Japanese Imperial system of Koki, 2598. Students wear both modern uniform and Korean dress (left, row 2), while the teacher sitting at front right wears Japanese kimono. The seven girls in row 2 may have combined with the boys' class for this graduation photo. (Norman Thorpe Collection)

came every week to our house, whether or not we subscribed to it. Worried that it would be discovered, my mother hid the papers to avoid suspicion.

It didn't help. The Japanese secret police knew we received that paper, so they assigned a police detective permanently to our house. Every morning the detective arrived and sat there in my father's office. All day. So we fed him, and gradually we got to be friends with him. After all, we were all humans. One detective we didn't like, but another one came and we got along with him just fine.

The only time I was conscious of being Korean was when my whole class went on a tour to Japan. We took a steamer from Shanghai to a southern port in Japan called Shimonoseki.

As soon as I got on board the boat, a detective from the Japanese secret police summoned me. I was frightened. I thought, I didn't do anything wrong. What can he want? This detective was not familiar to me. I had never seen him before.

He sat me down and asked me, what is your name, what does your father do, what do your brothers do, and so on. This is when I still had my Korean name.

I asked him back, "Why are you asking me these questions? Why only me?"

He said, "We are looking into something."

"What?" I asked.

"We have some suspicion about your father's ideology. It is not quite Japanese."

I answered, "He is only a scholar. I'm sure he is above suspicion."

I knew, and he knew, that among the Koreans in Shanghai, it was actually rare for Koreans to send their children to Japanese schools. Most Koreans sent their children to French schools, or Italian, American, or Chinese schools. So I told the detective, of all the schools my parents could have chosen, they sent me to a Japanese school. How can you say my parents are suspect?

I thought quickly. I told him that in Shanghai we often went to a Japanese bookstore called Uchiyama, whose owner, a Japanese, was a very close friend of my father. This owner respected my father highly, and he would say, "Professor Yu is a very learned man and there is a lot to learn from him." I told all this to the detective on the boat, and he finally let me go. I finished the tour with my classmates.

About 1938, when I was fourteen years old, with younger sisters in sixth grade and third grade, and a baby, my mother took us children back to Seoul to avoid the war in China. As soon as we arrived in Seoul, the police arrested my mother and took her away. We children went to the police station and all four of us stood in front of it and cried and cried. All that because they found a piece of that *Independence* newspaper as part of the wrapping paper around our packages. They were very thorough in searching. They kept demanding, did you read that newspaper?

We all denied having read it. We said that we found old newspaper to use in packing. We young ones certainly didn't know what this was all about.

My mother was quite a woman. She began fasting in jail to protest her false arrest. We took food to her and she did not touch any of it. She protested more strongly that we had gone all the way to Shanghai, paid a great amount of tax to Japan, and this was the reward she got. Finally they released her, but we really went through a hard time.

We returned to Shanghai and later, in 1943, I went to university in Tokyo. Already the air raids were unbelievably frequent. My parents, for the purpose of educating us, bought an apartment building in Tokyo for us to live in, but they were so worried, they kept saying, come back to Shanghai. So I left everything there and took the train from Tokyo to Shimonoseki and then a ship to Shanghai. We were afraid our boat might be sunk by American planes, but we made it safely.

My mother, however, wasn't so lucky. She died in November. She was on a trip from Shanghai to Shimonoseki and then to Pusan, and the ship was sunk by a B-29 bomber. That is how she died. To commemorate the victims of this bombing, a large funeral was held by the Korean community at the harbor in Hangchow, China, for those who perished in the water.

How many Koreans were like us under the Japanese—not resisting, just going along? Many went along, not by choice but because they had no other choice. Look how it worked. After the war, my family was branded *pro*-Japanese, but while we were *under* the Japanese my father was suspect and watched every day by a detective. How ironic.

EPILOGUE, 1945–1995

To escape being drafted into the Women's Service Corps, Miss Yu became engaged, and in November, on the first anniversary of her mother's death, she married. She and her husband raised five children, one of whom moved to America. When her husband retired, they joined their daughter in California. (For more details, see the entry for her husband, Yang Sŏngdŏk, in the appendix.)

11 : Becoming Japanese

Governor-General Minami Jiro, who ruled Korea from 1936 to 1942, believed that his historic mission was to achieve the complete union of Korea and Japan.[1] Among many other new rules, Koreans were now required to recite the Pledge of Imperial Subjects (1937), speak only Japanese (1938), worship at Shinto shrines (1939), and—the ultimate indignity—change their names to Japanese (1940).[2]

BOWING AT SHINTO SHRINES

Shinto ceremonies were not religious, the government said; they simply honored the Emperor. However, since the Japanese considered their Emperor a living god, his ancestors were also gods. Bowing at the shrines honored the living Emperor by honoring the hundreds and thousands of his god-ancestors.

Whether one attended the ceremonies appears to have depended on many factors. In some areas, police pressure to attend the shrines became severe, and coercion took many forms, from closing churches to denying food rations. Usually all government offices and schools required full group attendance, while workers in more private businesses or on farms may or may not have been coerced. Whether a specific place had a hilltop shrine or small shrines in workplaces and schools, and whether attendance was enforced, often depended on local situations and the personality of the local official. One elder said, "On the way to the shrine, I told my teacher I had something to do first. He said, 'All right, go ahead.' I always made excuses, and I didn't join that Shinto worship."

KANG SANG'UK [KANG SANG WOOK],
(m) b. 1935, physicist, North P'yŏngan Province:

The Japanese in almost every community set up Shinto shrines high on the hill and once a month they held a ceremony there. They ordered everyone, Japanese and Korean, to attend and bow to the gods of Shinto. The one in Kanggye city was quite large. Even though my family was Christian, I went along with the school group. We went during class hours and we kids trooped along without thinking too much about it.

Each village was supposed to have a shrine, but many villages were too small to bother with. Our ancestral village of Tŏktari never had Japanese people or a Shinto shrine. It was simply too small.

One Christian seminary told its people not to bow to the shrines and consequently they suffered continual persecution. Many others did as they were told in order to survive. As a child, I didn't notice all this. Mostly I played happily, drawing airplanes, drawing maps with different colors.

What did the shrine look like? As you walked up the hill, before you got to the shrine itself, you came to a red *torii* gate, just standing there. I mean, usually a gate serves as an opening in a wall, but there never was a wall, just the gate. It was big—wide enough for several of us to walk through side by side.

Farther up the hill, in a clearing where all of us could stand, was a little house very much like a small Buddhist temple, with the doors closed. From a building next door, the priest came out dressed in full regalia— very impressive, great robes and scepter—and he stood in front of the shrine. My teacher told us that inside was a statue of one of their goddesses, Amaterasu Omikami, the sun goddess, but I never actually saw inside. It was like the Holy of Holies, very sacred. The priest shouted, "Bow," and we all bent over from the waist with flat backs, and that's it, that's all. It was over. What took so long was you had to climb the hill and then walk back down.

KIM SUNOK, (m) b. 1910, fireman, Kyŏnggi Province:

When we rode the streetcar, passing through Seoul's South Gate, we passed directly in line of the Shinto shrine on Namsan. At noon even the streetcar stopped so we could bow in the direction of the shrine.

Shinto rites at a Korean school (probably Ŭnjin), 1930s. (Norman Thorpe Collection)

KIM YŎSŎNG, (m) b. 1910, photographer, Kyŏnggi Province:
They just made us do it. I had a photography business in Seoul, and they stopped by the shop and told us to go. Also, a notice came, addressed to the studio, telling us to go [to the Shinto ceremony].

YI OKPUN, (f) b. 1914, housewife, Kyŏnggi Province:
Of course we had to go up to the shrine on Namsan (South Mountain). The head of our neighborhood group was Japanese; that's why we had to do everything he said. If we didn't go, we didn't get any food ration.

We didn't go alone. A whole group went—our whole neighborhood cell, about ten households, you know. Even with my babies, I had to take the streetcar, then walk all the way up the hill. It was hard.

We had to go up a lot, sometimes once a week, certainly two or three times a month. The ceremony took about, let's see, thirty minutes. They pour some water, you clap your hands, then you come down and get the food ration stamps.

Later when we changed our name, I just followed whatever my husband said. I didn't care. Just get the food ration card!

SONG SŎKCHI, (m) b. 1916, businessman, Kyŏnggi Province:
Shinto shrine? I was just a businessman, I didn't work for a public entity, so personally, I never had to bow to Shinto gods. My father was deathly against it—he hated the Japanese and all things Japanese.

CH'OE KILSŎNG, (m) b. 1911, teacher, Kyŏnggi Province:
Schools, for sure, were forced to go as a whole group. As an individual, I didn't go, but as a teacher in the school, I had to go. No choice.

CH'U PONGYE, (f) b. 1913, housewife, South Kyŏngsang Province:
The Pusan shrine stood on top of the hill near the pier. We climbed up there many times, on holidays, but only for picnics. A beautiful view.

The Presbyterians held out for three years, but in September 1938, under unusual police pressure, they finally agreed to obey the edict. "Before the meeting of the assembly, each of the four hundred delegates was brought to a police station and told to vote for participation in the shrine ceremonies. When the session began, police officials sat facing the delegates; the police permitted no debate or negative votes. Whoever tried to leave the meeting was brought back by police escort. Under this pressure, the Presbyterian assembly resolved that the ceremonies were not religious."[3]

YI OKHYŎN, (f) b. 1911, housewife, Hwanghae Province:
Those who opposed going to the shrine expected prison and torture. Our church people felt terrible about it, but since we lived in a rural area, it didn't seem to be such a big issue.

Our pastor opposed Shinto worship, but the leaders went, anyway. They did that because the police said if we didn't bow, they would close the church. We didn't go very often, actually, just on days important to Japan.

My husband had to go. He had been in prison already and the police watched his every move. He'd come back and tell us that he had gone, but once there, he just said some bad things under his breath and came away.

KIM WŎN'GŬK [KIM WON KEUK], (m) b. 1918,
Tobacco Authority officer, North Hamgyŏng Province:
Our office didn't have a shrine, but it had a little altar of some sort. The first Monday of each month we had a morning assembly and bowed toward this altar by clapping our hands above our heads three times, and

Change by Coercion

then we bowed our heads. We did this, whether we believed or not. I really don't think many people believed any of it, Japanese or Korean, but if you didn't do it, it was too noticeable.

CHŎNG T'AE'IK, (m) b. 1911, farmer/lumberman, Kangwŏn Province:
I never, even in the mid-1930s, spoke a single word of Japanese. Also, I never went to a Shinto shrine. We were urged to go, but on our remote farm, and at our remote lumberyard, no one forced us, so we ignored it.

SCROLLS, OATHS, AND DECLARATIONS

The Japanese required Koreans to recite the "Pledge of the Imperial Subjects" at all public gatherings, whether religious, educational, or social.

> We are the subjects of the great empire of Japan.
> We shall serve the Emperor with united hearts.
> We shall endure hardships and train
> ourselves to become good and strong
> subjects of the Emperor.

KANG SANG'UK [KANG SANG WOOK],
(m) b. 1935, physicist, North P'yŏngan Province:
We lived in many different towns and I attended many different schools, but it was always the same. Every morning of every school day, sun, rain, or snow, we began with an assembly on the school grounds for attendance and announcements. Every single day the principal gave a homily and we all bowed east toward Tokyo and the Emperor and shouted "*Tenno Heika Ban Zai*"—"Long Live the Emperor."

About five or six times a year, on very exceptional occasions, they brought out a special scroll containing the Emperor's proclamation. Two such days were December 8 for the Declaration of the Second World War, and in April for Education Day.

The principal stood in front of us on a podium. The vice principal brought out the scroll in its lacquer box, elegantly wrapped with the chrysanthemum seal of the Japanese Emperor. He held the box high above his bowed head, eyes averted, wearing white gloves so his hands would not even touch the box. The principal, also wearing white gloves, received the scroll and read it reverently, then returned it to the vice principal. All of

Becoming Japanese

us kids were supposed to bow our heads and not look upon the sacred words of the Emperor, but of course we peeked.

Each of these special days had its own speech and we had to memorize them in civics class. The proclamations, of course, were totally serious. *Ch'in omoni* ("We the Emperor, consider") *wa ga* ("our") *k'o so k'o so* ("divine imperial ancestors").

But kids, you know, are not the least bit impressed with speeches, and we made games out of them. We stood facing each other with great ceremony, arms crossed over our chest, intoning heavily *"Ch'in omoni,"* throwing our arms wide to embrace the universe *"waaaaa ga"* and, surprise! one kid would quickly reach over and tickle the other under his outstretched arms *"k'o so k'o so, k'o so k'o so."* Gales of laughter!

When I was about nine and in fourth grade, we lived in Kanggye and actually had Japanese neighbors who also had fourth- and fifth-grade children, just like us. We became good friends, exchanged comic books, and went to each other's birthday parties. On rainy days we'd play marbles, and then we found out that in their own Japanese schools the kids also poked fun at the Emperor's speeches, but they, of course, didn't dare do it in public. They even did some things we hadn't thought of.

CH'OE KILSŎNG, (m) b. 1911, teacher, Kyŏnggi Province:
After the Second World War started, every morning during the morning assembly we bowed our heads toward the east where the Emperor was supposed to live, and we recited the oath. Our principal supervised this, but when he was away, I had to do it. When I had to direct the school to bow to the east, it really bothered me. I didn't like it at all. I'm not sure why, but inside I thought, you rascal, while outwardly I still had to bow my head.

NEW YEAR'S DAY

KIM P. [ANONYMOUS], (f) b. 1931, housewife:
The Japanese celebrated January 1 as their New Year's holiday, but we Koreans celebrated the lunar New Year several weeks later. In order to wipe out Korean customs, some Japanese teachers took their students on trips on the day of lunar New Year.

We might have a picnic or a work day. We might dig air-raid shelters or

Change by Coercion

hoe the farm rows, or weed a farmer's field. It should have been our holiday, but they took us far away from home so we could not celebrate as a family. It was on purpose, to break our traditional holiday.

KANG SANG'UK [KANG SANG WOOK],
(m) b. 1935, physicist, North P'yŏngan Province:
In the far north where I lived, the Japanese did not destroy our lunar celebration. At the lunar New Year we kids made a huge bonfire of rice straw. Only kids, no grownups. The grownups didn't mind because we were way out in the field. We went from house to house and begged good things to eat, then gathered back in the field and let loose all our excitement, yelling and jumping up and down in front of the bonfire.

On the night before the bonfire, we tried to stay awake all night long, because everyone knew that if you fell asleep on that night, your eyebrows would turn white. I remember putting white powder on my kid brother when he fell asleep.

CHANGING TO JAPANESE NAMES
In 1939, in order to bring about a "more perfect union," the government encouraged Koreans to abandon their Korean names and change both their family and personal names to Japanese. "The campaign was universal and intense, but no research has yet found an actual law to that effect. Rather it was a bureaucratic campaign. That may seem a trivial distinction when compared with the overall insult of the thing, but in fact, if people refused—and many did—the government had no legal recourse. The whole point was for the government to be able to say that the people had changed their names 'voluntarily.'"[4]

Of our fifty informants, only four families refused to change their names. All others complied, for without a Japanese name citizens could not enter schools, get jobs, or obtain ration cards. The government stopped issuing permits and postmen stopped delivering packages to those with Korean names. However, many Koreans built into their new names some ingenious reflection of their Korean name, hometown, or a significant family attribute.

PAK SŎNGP'IL,
(m) b. 1917, farmer/fisherman, South Kyŏngsang Province:
I got beaten up many times by the Japanese because I resisted changing my name to Japanese. Everybody around me changed theirs, but I had lost

my grandfather and then my father, and had taken over the responsibility of eldest son. That is why I tried not to change my name. But I got tired of being so badly beaten.

Out of desperation, I wrote to my aunt in Seoul, the one who had been arrested for the Independence demonstration. I asked her, should I do it? By return mail, she said, "Do you have *two fathers*? If you have two fathers, then change your name to the name of your Japanese father." She was furious!

So I held out a while longer, but I couldn't stand any more persecution. I finally changed my name to Otake. The *O* in Chinese characters is Korean *Tae*, the first syllable of the place where I was born. The *take*, meaning bamboo, is for the huge bamboo grove behind our house. So my name signified that I was born in Taebyŏn township in the house with the bamboo grove in back.

CHʼU PONGYE, (f) b. 1913, housewife, South Kyŏngsang Province:
We never changed our family name; we kept my married name of Pak. Our son did change his name to Parku Toshio, but my husband was very stubborn. My own family did not change their name, either. My brother, working in the city office, I don't know if he changed his name or not, but I'm sure he did it to keep his job. We saw each other often, back and forth, but did he tell me those things? No. He never told me about any hard times. He just minded his own business and didn't bother anybody.

YI CHAEʼIM, (f) b. 1919, housewife, Kyŏnggi Province:
My grandfather, the scholar, after we were forced to change names, was so upset he would not eat or even drink for many days.

KIM P. [ANONYMOUS], (m) b. 1924, township office worker:
I changed my name to Tomikawa, meaning "rich river." The characters in Korean read *Pu chʼŏn*. I chose the name myself. I had no particular reason, it just seemed like an easy name to pronounce. My grandfather objected, but since I was working, I had to change it. I am the only one in my family that did change, because all the others were still farmers. They didn't have to worry about losing their jobs.

Change by Coercion

YANG SŎNGDŎK,
(m) b. 1919, electrical engineer, South Ch'ungch'ŏng Province:
Every family had big discussions whether to go along or resist. My eldest brother, who took over the rice dealership, didn't change his name at all, because he was dealing mostly with other Koreans. But for those of us who had to go to school or get jobs, we had to come up with the new names.

This was just a tactic to make Koreans into Japanese. They didn't do this blindly, you know. They had very sinister plans. The purpose of changing names was obviously to make us sound Japanese, so that the younger generation would know nothing but the new names, and their thinking and their attitudes would become Japanese. This was all part of their long-range plan to eliminate any vestige of Korean consciousness.

KIM WŎN'GŬK [KIM WON KEUK],
(m) b. 1918, Tobacco Authority officer, North Hamgyŏng Province:
My clan had several meetings with lots of debate about whether to go along with the name change. Some were dead set against it, but finally after several meetings, they gave in.

I attended some of the meetings just to listen—I was too young to speak up. Those in favor said that without a Japanese name you could not do business with the Japanese, could not get jobs, could not send your children to school—in fact, could not do much at all. They said it was only a formality, our hearts were still Kim and we would always remain Kim. So we should just go along.

The patriarch of our local clan, an elder who commanded respect, at the third meeting, gave his opinion, which counted heavily. He said we should not draw undue attention to ourselves. Not stir up trouble. So the factions gave in and went along with the patriarch.

At least in our region, those who did not change their name to Japanese were the first targets of the draft to the factories.

Some Koreans took Japanese names in an arbitrary fashion, often defiantly illogical. In the name changes that follow, however, one can see the effort made by interviewees to hold on to their Korean heritage.

Korean Name Character and Meaning	Japanese Name and Meaning	Reason for Choice
Kim 金 gold	Kanekuni 金國 gold country	Retain "gold" 金 but use its Japanese pronunciation
	Kanezawa 金澤 gold pond	Retain "gold" 金 A popular Japanese name
	Kaneshiro 金城 gold castle	Retain "gold" 金
	Kaneda 金田 gold rice field	Retain "gold" 金
	Iwamoto 岩本 rock origin	We wanted a meaning to show our faith
Ch'oe 崔 山 = mountain	Yamamoto 山本 mountain origin	Ch'oe character is written with "mountain" on top, so we kept the mountain part
Pak 朴	Otake 大竹	"O" = "Tae" first syllable of the place where I was born. "Take" = bamboo. It signifies I was born in Taebyŏn township in the house with the bamboo grove in back.

Korean Name Character and Meaning	Japanese Name and Meaning	Reason for Choice
Pak 朴	Kido 木戸 wooden door	Kept the tree 木 from Pak
	Masaki 正木 Upright tree	Kept the tree 木 from Pak
Yi 李 木 = tree	Matsumoto 松本 Pine origin	Pine trees 松 are in Kyŏngju and Yi's clan is from Kyŏngju
	Kimoto 木元 Tree origin	Kept the tree from the top of Yi 木
Kang 康	Nobukawa 信川	Used the Chinese characters for the Kang ancestral seat which are read Sin ch'ŏn in Korean and Nobukawa in Japanese.
Kang 姜	Oyama 大山 Large mountain	Named after the mountain in the ancestral seat of his clan, read Tae san in Korean and Oyama in Japanese.

Korean Name Character and Meaning	Japanese Name and Meaning	Reason for Choice
Song 宋	Matsumoto 松本 Pine origin	The two characters 宋 and 松 and are both pronounced Song in Korean. The first one has no Japanese counterpart, so my brother took a character that sounded the same as our name and added the "moto" implying that Song, not the pine, but our Song, is the origin. Get it?

12 : Drafted to the Kobe Shipyards

CHŎNG CHAESU

Student (m) b. 1923, North Chŏlla Province

My father had one very unique skill—putting tiles onto roofs. In those days, tiles were set quite differently from today; it required a truly special skill. Obviously, rich people kept building houses, and they always wanted tile roofs, and they asked for Father because of his skill. But even rich people do not build houses every day, so sometimes we had money but mostly we didn't. It wasn't easy to live, because we had seven children and father refused other work.

Because our family was poor I paid for my own schooling, doing odd jobs to earn money. From fourth grade, I delivered the newspaper to pay for tuition and school supplies. I went up to Seoul for middle school, and because I had already paid for my own schooling, going up to Seoul did not faze me at all. I lived with my elder brother who was married and working in Seoul.

My draft call came on the first of October, 1944, when I was twenty-one. I wanted to run away, but my elder brother said, if that happens, the Japanese will give the rest of the family a hard time. So for the good of the family, he begged me to stay put and go when I was called up. The authorities said it would only be for one year. I told my brother, even one year is too long. I will run away. But he persisted.

The Japanese crowded us into a school ground in Seoul and then took us to Pusan. There were thousands of us, from all over the country, some in old-fashioned Korean clothes, some in modern dress. They put us on a ship. We had no idea where we were going.

We ended up in Kobe, Japan, where two large companies, Mitsubishi and Kawasaki, had their shipyards. The guards herded us into long barracks, located in a suburb of Kobe. Our group had six thousand Koreans, three thousand for Mitsubishi and three thousand for Kawasaki. All in those barracks. Can you imagine?

For meals we ate beans, beans, and more beans. No white rice, ever. It just didn't exist. Sometimes they gave us a small bowl of soup. Even at that, they doled out small portions. We were young and hungry and full of appetite. How can you get by with that food when you are only twenty-one? In desperation some tried to sneak more food, and then they were beaten. Severely! I just couldn't bear it.

Each barrack had Japanese officers assigned to it, all judo or martial arts experts, to keep order among these energetic young people. The guards gave each of us one drab brown uniform to wear to work. We changed into our own clothing when we got back to our ward, but some men did not have a change of clothing. They stayed in their uniforms day and night. Those uniforms became black. For laundry, we went to the nearby river and washed by hand. Very primitive.

We had one day off, when we could go into the nearby town, but even with money, things were so scarce there wasn't much to buy. Money was of no use.

At Kobe harbor, the city spread along the seashore, and the United States military bombed the city systematically, section by section. Everything became like charcoal, black, sooty. Bombs weren't the only thing. Sometimes, they strafed us with machine guns.

When the B-29s dropped bombs, the damage was not so great, but when incendiary bombs fell, the damage was enormous. When those bombs first dropped, the guards told us that if one dropped on our ship, we should pick it up and throw it in the sea! But they soon saw that when that bomb drops, it breaks into small pieces and spreads like wild fire. You can't get away. The fire runs after you.

I really didn't feel much danger because the bombs dropped in the city and I worked in the harbor. So I watched those incendiary bombs dropping on the city. After the night shift, in the morning, we saw what had happened to the city—the fire so white hot that even iron bars were bent out of shape. We saw houses all burned. Some people who had gone into a

Change by Coercion

bomb shelter were burned to death even there, burned so badly that you couldn't tell if it was a man or woman. The damage was extraordinary.

WORKING ON THE SHIP

We worked on a huge military ship, camouflaging it from the American planes. When they took it off dry dock we finished the top and the inside. This work had to be done deep in the bottom of the ship. The workers banged away with rivets and machinery, making huge noises that reverberated inside the ship. Those workers went down in the morning and came out late at night. They never saw the sun. The black dust flew around in there and covered them with soot, so they were all black—their whole bodies, all black.

The officer on board ship chose me to be his deputy and ordered me to take refreshments to the other officers and guards. Because of that, I didn't suffer too badly. Part of my job was to deliver lunches to the Japanese guards. In their box lunch they had white rice and other tasty things, but even so, these bosses were so spoiled that they complained about the quality of their food. They yelled, "This is not fit for human consumption. Not even pigs would eat this!" They actually tossed it to me, and yelled, "Here, *you* eat this."

When they did that, I shared it with my friends because they were really starving. The rest I stashed away, dried it, hid it, so I could take it with me when I got ready to escape. I did this for several months.

Prisoners of war worked there also, mixed in with us. These prisoners were mostly British, captured in Singapore. You could tell they had been starved—they were just skin and bones. They looked so emaciated that even we, who were hungry, thought they looked starved. They were brought to the ship in shackles, then the shackles were taken off. They scrounged in the garbage cans for any scraps of food.

I felt so sorry for them that I shared cigarettes in secret. They said to me, thank you, thank you, so many times that I felt embarrassed for the little I could do. If I had been caught, of course, my own life would be in danger. Although we couldn't really communicate, whenever they saw me they smiled, laughed, and called out. There is no question that some things that one human being should never do to another had been done by those Japanese.

Now remember, even though we had so little food, we were all young, full of passion and vigor. So if a fellow Korean suffered, we all rallied around him and had at it with the Japanese, so really, they were afraid of us.

I was twenty-one, and I had a strong righteous conviction, an idealistic passion, and one day it sparked an uproar. My officer assigned to me a young Korean boy who didn't speak Japanese. One day, the boy and I had to take a box lunch to the ship's captain, and we had to walk past the guards. These guards came mostly from the underground organization called *yakuza*, because these gangsters were not allowed into the regular army—even the Japanese shunned them as impure. However, the police hired them to be guards for prisoners. These fellows really knew how to fight. Now, you need to know that when we went past one of these guards, we were supposed to say, in Japanese, "Pardon me," and then pass him. You also had to bow a little bit.

Since this young boy didn't speak Japanese, he didn't do this, and the guards considered it the height of disrespect and rudeness. They beat him up—they settled everything with beatings! They also, can you believe it, threw the lunch intended for the captain into the sea.

I ran up to them and yelled, "He cannot speak Japanese yet, that's why he didn't say it! He didn't mean to be rude. You have to tell him, teach him a phrase or two. Don't just beat him up."

Then, of course, they turned on me. I knew I should not fight back, but I was young and strong, and my emotion just took over. I beat *them* up. Somehow, the word spread that a Korean was being beat up, and *hundreds* of my fellow workers came up from the bottom of the ship and converged on the deck. Think of it—a regular gang fight! The prisoners just needed something to stir them to action, an outlet for all their frustrations.

Somehow we got separated and the fight ended. Then the *yakuza* came after me with huge wooden clubs, looking for me all over the ship because I was the one who challenged them. But to them, all us Koreans looked alike, they couldn't tell us apart, so they couldn't find me.

My platoon leader and the captain had both taken a liking to me, so instead of all of us being punished, they just said they would let the incident go. In fact they were solicitous toward me. They said that I should be wary of those guards, that we all knew they were low class, unruly, and we knew they were hired only because all the regular army was at the front fighting. Our Japanese bosses actually took our side against the *yakuza*. Looking back, I am amazed at my gumption, to stand up to them and get into that fight. I wonder sometimes what possessed me.

My worst memory is the misery there in Kobe. Those three thousand guys in the shipyard at Kobe, when the bombers came over or machine guns strafed us, some of the Koreans actually ran out into the open. To show how ignorant they were, they said the bombers would not shoot at Koreans, they would only bomb the Japanese. Some of them looked up directly into the machine gun fire. I yelled to them, "Get inside! Hide!"

The machine guns spit fire, really, really awful. When it hit the human body, the flesh just blew off, and then these blown-off pieces of flesh splattered against the walls. It was ghastly. We watched in horror. When I saw those things, it added to my determination to escape.

ESCAPE

I heard that a spy network existed among the Koreans and that if I could get to a certain place, boats would take me to the eastern coast of Korea. On the other hand, if I was caught, I'd be executed.

I told my friends, if I get caught I'll die, but if I stay here under these conditions I am going to die anyway. So I am going to take a chance and run away. If anybody wants to come with me, it's the time to come, because I'm leaving. Well, two guys joined me.

On the 24 of July, 1945, I reported in sick and took the day off. Then I went to the cafeteria and told the cook that I'd like to go outside a bit. He prepared a box lunch for me, and then we ran away in broad daylight.

At the shore, we stole a little boat and rowed our way out to sea. Soon the sea patrol came alongside to check on us. I showed them a fake travel permit I had made and told them that we had to go to point B, and perhaps they could help us get there. They fell for the story and helped us. Then we just wandered the ocean for about five days, looking for the smuggling ship on the other side of the main island, because we had no idea where it was.

We ended up at a small port called Hamamatsu. With amazing good luck we got hooked up with a Korean. He told us that if we went to Senzaki we would find the ship to Korea.

That meant we would have to go overland. On the way, we stopped by a field and asked the elderly farmers working there to please give us potatoes because we were so hungry. They felt sorry for us and gave us food, telling us that their own sons were taken to the front, and they hadn't heard anything about them, and so they felt close to us because we were their sons' age. They were good to us.

We got to Senzaki and hid in a cow stall for two days waiting to board the ship. While we waited, the secret police came. The Korean owner of the cow stall told us that since the police kept coming, suspecting something, we must go hide someplace else.

We left the house and took the train for one hour to a town called Shomeiji. We put up in a fleabag inn, but the police came and checked our identification. Now remember, we did have a fake travel permit and it said we had to gather food supplies to take back to Kobe. Well, they searched our bags, asking, what is in there?

I said, "It only contains the food for us for several days and a change of clothes."

"Is it true?" they asked.

"Of course," we said.

"Well, all right. But show up at the police station at a certain time this evening."

We said yes, we would, but as soon as those police were out of sight, we took off. We managed to get back to the house and pleaded with the man to put us back in the cow stall because it was even more dangerous outside. He protested, but he let us stay.

Finally we found that boat. We paid seventy yen each to the Korean captain, and at one o'clock in the middle of the night we got under way.

Now, this was a fishing boat, and the captain told us to go down to the very bottom of the boat where the fish were. The stink was awful. We couldn't breathe. When we got down to the bottom of the ship, we found more than thirty fellows there, crammed in with the fish!

They told us to be quiet, to not say a single word. It was terrible—the stink, the noise of the engine. After about five hours of this, about six in the morning, they said we could come up to the deck. Whew. We asked how long it took to get to Korea. They said about fifteen hours.

But fifteen hours came with no sight of land. Twenty hours came and still no land. It turned out that this boat was so small, it bounced like a leaf in a storm and the high waves kept pushing it back. Those waves went this way and the boat drifted that way, and sometimes the engine even stopped.

I had been trained to fix engine parts, so I helped out restarting the engine, over and over. The others all got seasick because of the rolling, so they gave absolutely no help at all.

We had no idea how long we drifted out there. Hours and hours. Finally, we spotted a shape on the horizon. We imagined we saw white clothes moving and said, white clothes, Koreans wear white clothes, we must be in Korean waters. We drifted to land and arrived at a small seashore village near Ulsan. We learned we had been at sea for forty-six hours. We didn't eat all that time—seasick—such violent waters.

Luck kept with me at every turn. To this day, I still can't figure out how I had the gumption to run away and do all those things that I did to get home to Korea.

EPILOGUE, 1945–1995

After the Japanese left Korea, Mr. Chŏng operated a factory in Pusan making military underwear for the army and navy. During the Korean War he established a cemetery for the U.S. military personnel killed in Korea, and when that war ended, he resumed supplying uniforms to the Korean military, but moved to Seoul. When he retired, he moved to America at the invitation of his children.

13 : The War Effort

The Second World War raged, and Japan needed help. First they engaged Koreans in labor draft (*ching yong*), forcing men, women, and children to collect war donations, join "voluntary" labor corps, and work in mines, construction sites, and factories. Toward the end of the war, the military draft (*ching byŏng*) policy put Korean men into armed fighting units. Against this, whenever possible, Koreans continued their passive resistance by hiding, ignoring the summons, or finding essential home-front jobs. More often, no loopholes existed and no escape was possible.

THE DRAFT

CHŎNG KŬMJAE [CHUNG KUM JAE],
(m) b. 1919, day laborer, North Ch'ungch'ŏng Province:
During 1944 and 1945 I got four labor draft notices. Each time, I hid and they never enforced the notice. At least in my area, they just had to fill a quota. If some men didn't show up, they grabbed others. Finally the war was over and I never had to go.

KIM P. [ANONYMOUS], (m) b. 1924:
I received the military draft notice, but I really didn't want to go into the army. I was married and we had a child, but that didn't make any difference to the Japanese. They wanted all the help they could get.

Somebody said, why don't you go to a fortune teller to get advice? So I went. He told me to run away because my lot as a soldier would be a very bad one. I took his advice and went to my aunt several villages away. I stayed in hiding for six months and twenty days and then the war was over.

My parents got into trouble because I ran away. The police went to my house every single day, demanding to know where I had gone. Sometimes the police went, sometimes the township officials, asking the same things over and over.

I didn't hide in the attic or in the woods, I just tried to stay indoors because the Japanese questioned any young man seen on the street. At that time, every young man should be in the army or on a work team. My fake document said I was on official travel, and I used that whenever I ran into a roadblock or had to show identification.

YI SŬNGBONG, (m) b. 1912, tailor, Kyŏnggi Province:
The shop where I worked, Hasegawa tailor shop, was one of the few large ones in Seoul, large enough that the colonial government ordered uniforms from us. I was the supervisor under the Japanese owner but I never socialized with the boss. He just came in every day, sat around and swatted flies. Toward the end of the war, when many were drafted into the army and to the mines, we were spared. The owner of our shop found some way to protect us all from the forced military draft.

YI OKPUN, (f) b. 1914, housewife, Kyŏnggi Province:
They sent my husband to Nagasaki, to a coal mine. He was gone about a year. While he was away, we really had a hard time. Aigo, it was hard. If it hadn't been for my mother's mother, on the farm where I grew up, coming up to Seoul and bringing with her some rice and other farm produce, we really would have starved. In those days, there were a lot of checkpoints and they were very careful and checked everything, but grandmother somehow got past them all and brought us food.

SIN KWANGSŎNG, (m) b. 1915, farmer, North Kyŏngsang Province:
They drafted me to labor in early spring 1945. They just said, "*You* and *you* have to go." They sent me to work in a mine in Kyushu, Japan, but I got sick and they sent me back to my hometown.

When I regained my health, they drafted me again. This second time they sent me to a pipe factory in Saitama prefecture. People said, "Oh, it is so dangerous," but I found that it was not really so dangerous. Physically, I mean. They paid us a tiny, tiny salary. I sent it all home to my family. The mine where I was before had been safe, but at this Saitama factory there were many B-29 bombing raids. We had to quit working every time there was a raid and go into a bomb shelter.

They told us that the Americans had invented a new weapon and when the Americans invaded the mainland, we would all die gloriously. We made sharp bamboo spears so we could stab the Americans when they came.

KIM WŎN'GŬK [KIM WON KEUK],
(m) b. 1918, Tobacco Authority officer, North Hamgyŏng Province:
In 1943 I transferred to work in Ch'ŏngjin, a town on the eastern coast in the far, far north. The supervisor looked like a typical Japanese, but he did not talk or act typical. He disliked discriminatory practices against the Koreans, and so he treated everybody the same. He was famous for that in our area. His favorite criticism against his fellow Japanese was, "We Japanese have a narrow island mentality, but we are nothing but a little frog in a little pond. We do not have the big picture in mind."

When I first heard him say that to me, I was afraid to take him seriously. I thought he was tricking me into saying something against the Japanese. So I was cautious and wary. Gradually, I came to believe him.

That summer a group from our bureau got assigned a war effort job and spent three weeks refurbishing an airfield outside of Ch'ŏngjin. We carried away rocks, smoothed out the runway surfaces—all physical labor. Different groups worked three-week shifts. Once a year, our group had to do this. We lived at home and just went there during the day instead of going to our regular jobs.

In the middle of this work, my Japanese supervisor and I went out to have dinner and drinks together. When he had some liquor under his belt, he started muttering, "This airfield we are building, after we are defeated, it may become a Russian airfield or even an American airfield. So why are we working so hard, building it?"

It surprised me to hear this, but I hesitated to agree. I still didn't trust myself to say anything against Japan. This topic you didn't dare mention in front of even the most friendly Japanese.

SONG SŎKCHI, (m) b. 1916, businessman, Kyŏnggi Province:
The colonial government formed Bombing Recovery Groups whose members were exempt from the draft. Their job was to organize the neighborhood cell families and lead the cleanup effort if American bombers came.

I was appointed the head of the Neighborhood Association Group in my area of Seoul. Whenever an American bomber, or even the hint of one, flew overhead, we gathered at a preassigned place and waited until the all-clear signal, any time, day or night. If our neighborhood cell got bombed, we were responsible to do what we could for recovery. I was a foreman. Below me, Koreans could get the positions. Above me were a supervisor and a chief, both Japanese.

KANG SANG'UK [KANG SANG WOOK],
(m) b. 1935, physicist, North P'yŏngan Province:
The Second World War was going on, and up in the far north we thought the United States was going to start bombing us. Planes did fly over, and that silver streak in the blue sky, I remember, was so pretty.

Whenever those planes came, the school had an air raid and sent the students home. So we children asked, "Are we going to have an air raid today?" You know how kids are, they don't want to study. Well, I didn't learn much during those days. Sometimes the planes came at ten in the morning and we'd go home. So every day we'd trudge to school saying, "I wish we'd have an air raid; I'd have all day to play."

COMFORT WOMEN
Thousands of young, unmarried Korean women were mobilized into the Voluntary Service Brigade and told they would help the war effort as nurses or factory workers. Instead, they found themselves taken to "comfort stations" at the war front and expected to provide sexual services for the soldiers. If they refused, they were beaten and denied food. After the war, the shame of being a "comfort woman" kept these women silent, and only recently have they begun to tell their stories.

Most of the women who talked with us said they never heard of "comfort women" when they were young. "I guess it was because I lived in such an urban area," one said. "They didn't collect girls in big towns." Others said they were too young to hear about it, or too far removed from the mainstream. One woman hinted at another possibility—the girls simply never learned the truth until it was too late.

KIM P. [ANONYMOUS], (f) b. 1931, housewife:
Some things were bad and you just learned to avoid them if you could. My aunt was only seventeen, but she had to hurry up and get married to avoid being drafted. It wasn't the "comfort women," but some sort of war effort group. If you were married you didn't have to go.

KIM PONGSUK, (f) b. 1924, housewife, Kyŏnggi Province:
When I was about twenty, the local Neighborhood Association—the watchdog group, spy network, channel for government rules and dictates—came to verify my age and marital status.

I had no choice but to acknowledge that I was young, single, and living at home. The next thing I knew, the local police came and summoned me to appear at the elementary school yard on a certain date.

A lot of other girls got called also, all about the same age, and the Japanese told us that we would serve the Emperor and the great cause of the Japanese empire by becoming nurses and taking care of the Imperial Japanese soldiers. They told us that the pay would be very good and we would be well taken care of. Some girls were really very excited about doing this.

We were to be sent to the front, but to do that we needed training. They gave each of us a wooden rifle and we had to practice. I kept thinking, I'm a woman. Why do I need this rifle? The rifle had a pretend bayonet and we had to plunge it into a straw "person" on the ground, again and again.

I hated this! I didn't want to do it. My parents decided I should get married, and then I wouldn't have to go. So I obeyed my parents and got married, and it turned out to be a fortunate thing. Much later, I found out that the women who went overseas to the front were forced into being comfort women. Japanese called these *Teishintai*, meaning "Volunteer Corps."

I also know about them because my husband met many Korean women serving the soldiers in Manchuria when he was drafted into the Japanese army and sent to the front line. Being married helped me but it didn't help him. He was taken only a few months after our marriage.

Military training of students (probably Ŭnjin School), 1930s.
(Norman Thorpe Collection)

My husband, having just married me and missing me, and also seeing that these comfort women were Korean women of the same age as me, when his turn came to go in to them, his physical desire was there, but he kept thinking of me, and he didn't do it.

The men lined up outside the barracks doors where the women were, and took their turn. The girl just lay there inside. Each man had a given amount of time, about seven minutes. If he wasn't out in time, the next man went right in and yanked him out. Each door had a long line of men waiting their turns. But when my husband's turn came, he just couldn't go in and do it.

The woman, on the wall near her head, used chalk or a pencil to make a mark for each soldier she serviced. She thought she would be paid that way, but it turned out they were not paid anything at all.

All this I heard from my husband in Manchuria.

WOMEN AND CHILDREN IN THE WORKFORCE

Each neighborhood group formed a Women's Association to support the war. Once a month they met, and as a group, went out to the fields to work, collected materials for the war effort, sewed towels, or stitched encouraging words in black characters onto small towels.

For students in junior and senior high school, part of their school day became a time of forced labor, right in the schoolroom or outside in factories or in the countryside. This work went on during the school year and also during vacation.

KIM SŎBUN, (f) b. 1914, housewife, South Kyŏngsang Province:
Rumor had it that some soldiers were saved because they had our towels wrapped around their chests and the towels stopped some bullets. Very seriously, we sewed them.

I met many Japanese women because of that group. In fact, after the war, when they were leaving Korea, many of these wives left their belongings to me because we had become friends.

One thing always bothered me. When the Japanese wives talked to each other, they used the phrase *Oku-san*, but when they talked to me, those same Japanese wives said *Okami-san*, consistently. That is a slightly lower level of address. One time I confronted one of the women and said, "Why do you call me that lower title?" She had no reply. Both phrases mean the same thing as Korean *ajumŏni*, or English *Mrs.*, but they are different levels.

There were many subtle things like that—you just had to ignore them most of the time.

PAK C. [ANONYMOUS], (f) b. 1927, housewife:
What did we do? We sewed uniforms, making the leggings that the Japanese soldiers wore from ankle to knee, and punching holes in leather things so that others could sew them. We found it terribly difficult to drill holes in the leather. There was no machine. They gave us a sharp tool to punch the holes by hand and many times our fingers got bloody. One time I pricked my finger so badly I still imagine I feel the pain.

They told us that in a crisis we would be sent to the front lines to help care for the injured, or do any other tasks necessary to fight the holy war. To prepare for that, they sent us to a hospital in P'yŏngyang to learn about first aid, putting on bandages, caring for light injuries, and things like that.

One time we witnessed an actual surgery operation for uterine cancer. It was full of blood and I was too queasy to watch. I hunkered in the back of the group. Once, the doctor cut out and displayed to us, his arm raised high, a huge tumor that he had cut out. It was horrid.

PAE YŎNG'OK, (f) b. 1929, housewife, North P'yŏngan Province:
I attended Chŏng-ŭi High School in P'yŏngyang. It was a Methodist
mission school, but by the time I went there, the missionaries had all been
sent away.

From the second year of high school (eighth grade), the teachers
taught less and less and we students worked more and more. After the
morning assembly we had about two hours of class, then lunch, and then
devoted the entire afternoon to making cotton gloves and other things for
soldiers.

The teachers brought in the materials. We students sat at our desks and
had to sew them. There were no sewing machines and it was very, very
hard to push the needles through the rough material. We were only young
girls. It hurt.

Depending on how productive we were, we got better grades. Still,
some girls just couldn't do it, even bribed with good grades. Their hands
would bleed and get blisters.

We continued to do this every day until the end of the war, through the
third year of school.

CHIN MYŎNGHŬI, (f) b. 1932, housewife, South Hamgyŏng Province:
Things were all right until 1942, when I was in fifth grade. Our city of
Wŏnsan was a harbor, so in the morning I had classes and in the afternoon
for two hours, our whole school marched to the factory to can fish that
were caught right there along the coast.

The cannery was huge, with row upon row of building after building.
They were supposed to dry the fish, but first the fish had to be pounded. So
for two hours every afternoon, we had to go pound the fish. Kids came to
work from every school, boys and girls, from fifth grade up to middle
school. It was hot and my arms ached, but we couldn't stop.

In winter they couldn't dry the fish, so then, three times a week they sent
us into the hills to collect pine tree sap. Year in and year out we did this—
1943, 1944, 1945.

When it rained, we learned how to give first aid and make bandages, and
we practiced running to the air-raid shelter in the hill behind the school.
Even the holes in the hill were dug by students, but not by me.

I graduated from sixth grade in March 1945, and in April I entered a

Methodist mission school. All the missionaries were gone by then, sent to prison camps. Here, after the morning assembly, there were no classes. We knew that the war in Europe was over, so just Japan was fighting—nobody could study. Again, we all trooped over to the factories to pound those awful fish.

14 : *Mansei*

KOREA FOREVER—TEN THOUSAND YEARS

In the summer of 1945, rumors chased each other through the air. People listened and watched but dared not comment.

August 7 (or August 6 in western hemisphere), America bombed Hiroshima; August 9 (or August 8), Russia declared war on Japan, and Russian airplanes attacked the Korean city of Ch'ŏngjin in North Hamgyŏng Province; August 10 (or August 9), America bombed Nagasaki; and by August 15 (or August 14) Japan surrendered and Korea was released from Japanese control.

KIM WŎN'GŬK [KIM WON KEUK], (m) b. 1918, Tobacco Authority officer, North Hamgyŏng Province:
That summer, rumors were like leaves on the trees—falling everywhere. I had been working about two years at Ch'ŏngjin, right on the east coast in the far north, and by July of 1945 we all felt uneasy, without really knowing why.

On the morning of August 9, Russia declared war on Japan, and Russian airplanes attacked the city of Ch'ŏngjin. Everything went into chaos. On the eleventh, communication to Seoul was severed. We couldn't get through. We were on our own. Isolated.

Now I really got worried. I felt compelled to get away from this border town. My Japanese superior also wanted to flee, so he wrote his own permission to travel, saying it was for discussions with headquarters. He authorized himself to go.

He had only been in this northernmost town for a few months, and was completely unfamiliar with the area. He relied on me for advice and assis-

*Government postcard published August 15, 1946, to celebrate the first anniversary
of liberation from Japanese rule. Note the chains and Japanese flag underfoot.
(Norman Thorpe Collection)*

tance, and he helped me in return. Right then, he gave me false travel papers and told me that I should go to my hometown, Sŏngjin, on the coast farther south. So we both made our plans to leave on the 13 of August. My wife agreed that I should get away while I had this chance, and she would follow with our two children as soon as she could.

I knew the man at the train station, and he told me to be at the station in the morning with my luggage. I took eight pieces of luggage to the station and gave them to my station friend to load on the train when it came. Suddenly I ran into my boss bringing his own luggage on a horse cart. We were happy to see each other and he pleaded with me to ask my station friend to put his luggage on the train, also.

I told him that, to compensate the man, he should sell him three cartons of cigarettes, way beyond the ration amount. If he could do that, the station man surely would try to help. So my boss said yes and I ran back to the office and got the cartons. It made the station worker very happy.

However, the train did not come in the morning. It did not come all day long. It finally came at eleven o'clock at night, in the pitch-black night, with all the lights doused to avoid an air raid. To our surprise, every possible space was crammed with wounded Japanese soldiers! Even more soldiers stood right there in our own town square waiting to get on. Many, many waited. There was no space for civilians at all.

To understand what happened next, you need to know that the train tracks in that corner of the country make a huge loop to three stations up in the farthest northeast corner of Korea, and then come back to our town before heading straight south. At each of those northern stations the train picked up more wounded soldiers! So even when the next train came round, early the next morning, we still couldn't get on. I learned too late not to be greedy—with my eight pieces of luggage there was just no room for me. Between my Japanese boss and myself, we had nineteen pieces of luggage.

In normal times, the laborers at the station would help load our luggage onto the train, but in the panic of that awful night, they all disappeared and we had to do it ourselves. Of course, besides the crush of soldiers, many civilians besides us waited there, pleading, yelling, pushing, shoving, trying to get on that train. Soldiers, with mock rifles made of wood, beat the people back to keep them from getting on. It was chaos.

We two stood together, watching and waiting. Seeing the turmoil, my boss said, "Young Kaneda [my Japanese name], let's forget it. Let's just run away."

"What about our luggage?" I asked. "It will be stolen."

So we stood around, not knowing what to do.

Another train came at ten o'clock. Again we tried to get on, but still there was no room. The train was totally full from the three stations in the loop before us. Even the windows were locked to keep people out.

I saw that one car, right behind the locomotive, was open. That's where the post office bags were stacked. My station worker friend said I should go around in front of the locomotive to the other side, and then I could get in that car. So I dragged some of my luggage with me, but there was not a speck of room—the load was already up to the ceiling.

I shoved myself and one suitcase up on top. The engineer said, "I warn you. If you get off the train to load any more luggage, you won't be able to get on again. Make up your mind. Stay with that one piece you are sitting on, or risk being left behind. Forget that other fellow if you want to live."

Right then the train began moving. There I was, alone, and could not even say goodbye to my boss who was still on the other side of the train, sitting with all the rest of the luggage. To this day, I feel bad that I could never explain to him what happened. He must believe that I betrayed him.

On August 15 I ran into a classmate and he told me that Japan had surrendered! I could not believe it.

KANG SANG'UK [KANG SANG WOOK],

(m) b. 1935, physicist, North P'yŏngan Province:

In August 1945, my elder sister and I spent the summer vacation from primary school at Grandmother's house in Tŏktal village, North P'yŏngan Province.

I know exactly where I was, lazily painting a watercolor picture on the porch of Grandmother's Big House (the tile-roof house of the village elder) in the hot afternoon, half listening to the buzz of the women at the well. Out of the afternoon haze, I heard one of them telling of a rumor she heard, that the Japanese had just surrendered and the Second World War was over. The Japanese rule of Korea was over? I jumped up and ran to Grandmother to ask if it was true.

The grownups cried and carried on, and the next day everyone from our village walked down the road to Chŏngju city to join an emotional celebration.

When vacation ended, Sister and I left Grandmother's and returned to our family in the border town of Pyŏkdong, far up the Yalu River. Now that we had no Japanese rulers, Father quickly transferred himself back to manage the bank in our hometown of Chŏngju. Within two months we packed and left that remote border area.

We drove away in a rickety open truck, five children and all our belongings crammed in the back. I remember that it burned wood for fuel, not gasoline. We worked our way out of that remote, wild country, slowly creeping down steep mountain roads, trying not to lose anything or anybody as the truck swung around the narrow mountain switchbacks.

Life for the Japanese changed overnight. In our Chŏngju area, our people policed themselves, and treated the Japanese well. The Japanese went to live in shelters or schools, and went out during the day to find jobs. We ourselves hired a Japanese woman as our maid.

One man who had been the middle-school principal was reduced to living at the shelter and going out during the day to seek work. One day two boys saw him and they thought he looked familiar. When they got close and recognized their former principal, old habits took over. They automatically stopped and gave him their respectful bow, even though he now dressed as a rag picker. He returned their bow, and right there shed tears, to think that the boys still respected who he was, not what he had become.

As for me, one day, walking toward Tŏktal village to visit Grandmother, I noticed a Japanese family trudging dejectedly along the road in the opposite way, toward Chŏngju city. I gasped when I recognized the school principal and his family from Chŏnch'ŏn where we had lived earlier. They had been our friends. I didn't know what to do. I hung my head and pretended I didn't see them. To this day I am ashamed that I couldn't even greet them.

In our north part of the country, when the Japanese packed up to leave, no one really knew how to rule in their place. People tried to police themselves and in some areas it worked better than others. Where we lived, in Chŏngju, it was calm and orderly. Much later I learned that terrible things happened in some places, especially in Hamgyŏng Province to the northeast near the Russian border. Anti-Japanese nationalists let out all their frustrations, and also the Korean communists, who had been biding their time, became militant. Cruel guerrilla attacks made everyone nervous. Nobody really knew who was in charge.

My family had one minor experience with these fears. After we returned to Chŏngju, one day as we visited Grandmother in Tŏktal, a messenger came running, crying out that a guerrilla band was headed our way. He didn't know for sure which kind of band. So everyone in the tiny hamlet ran from their houses and we all headed up into the mountain to hide. We huddled together, scared, trying to keep the children quiet and out of earshot of the houses below. We waited and waited. We had no idea if it was safe to return. After several hours we were so tired that one person went down to scout around. He came back to say it appeared to be a false alarm. We all went home and that was it.

CHŎNG T'AE'IK [CHUNG TAE IK],
(m) b. 1911, farmer/lumberman, Kangwŏn Province:
During those last years of the Japanese occupation, I ran a lumber business in Kangwŏn Province, cutting down trees from the mountains and selling them for lumber. I had just gotten an order for many trees to be sent to Japan, and my job was to transport them to the south where they could be shipped to Japan.

By the end of July, I had the logs all loaded in Wŏnju, and I watched the freight train start on its way south. I took the passenger train down to Pusan and planned to meet the logs when they arrived. I arranged everything with my Japanese counterpart, who had ordered the logs. In Pusan, we waited for the freight train to arrive, loaded with the trees. When it arrived he would pay me.

We waited three weeks. Every day I went to Pusan station to see if my freight train had arrived, and it never came. It should have taken only a few days.

I had no idea at the time what was holding up my train. It turned out that the Japanese knew they were losing the war, and all up and down Korea they diverted any "non-essential" freight to sidelines to let the military trains get through.

While I sat there waiting for my lost train, the Japanese Emperor announced his surrender and the trains stopped completely! I lost everything. I had no idea where along the lines I might find my logs. Not only that,

Change by Coercion

there were no trains at all for civilians, and I had to walk—*walk!*—all the way from Pusan back to Kangwŏn Province [250 miles].

CHIN MYŎNGHŬI, (f) b. 1932, housewife, South Hamgyŏng Province:
My father had lived in both Russia and Japan. When he returned to Korea, he got a job teaching in Wŏnsan, South Hamgyŏng Province, and became principal, which was very unusual for a Korean. Almost always, school principals were Japanese.

Because of Father's high position, we lived in a Japanese neighborhood and my best friends were Japanese. I did not know or use any Korean language at all, not speaking or reading or writing.

After liberation, the Koreans said my father was pro-Japanese, a running dog, because he was so high up. They almost lynched him. Then the Russian army came, and they wanted someone who could speak Russian to help them out. Father said no. So because of these two events, he fled to south Korea, leaving the rest of the family in the north. Later we made our own way to the south.

KIM P. [ANONYMOUS], (f) b. 1931, housewife:
When the war ended, everyone stopped using Japanese and started speaking Korean again. I was young, and I had never spoken Korean in my entire life. Since I didn't know a single word of Korean, I repeated the sixth grade just to learn to speak my own native language.

YU TŎKHŬI, (f) b. 1931, housewife, South Ch'ungch'ŏng Province:
I noticed that the Second World War upset the entire social order of our village. My uncle had many servants and they all knew their places, but when the war required the young men to be drafted into the Japanese army, every young man was taken, servants and *yangban*, all went together, and it blurred the hierarchy. Everybody's fate was the same, so they all became equal. Because of that, after the war, many of the servants moved out of Uncle's house and moved to other cities. The old order crumbled.

PAK SŎNGP'IL, (m) b. 1917, fisherman, South Kyŏngsang Province:
On August 15, I finished ferrying doctors out to the troop ship in the Pusan harbor, docked my boat, and went upstairs in the office building. I had no idea what had happened. I saw the Japanese workers in the office

wailing, banging on the desks, banging the floor. I can see them today in my mind. These very ones who had been so sure they were invincible. The next thing they did was drink themselves into a stupor. They went crazy. It was the tragedy of a nation in defeat.

KIM HOJUN, (m) b. 1918, farmer, Hwanghae Province:
My father-in-law, as vice-mayor, had to spearhead the collection of all that metal—the bronze bowls and candlesticks, dishes, pots, pans, kettles, rings. He was pro-Japanese, for sure.

When the Japanese left, my father-in-law barely escaped with his life. He knew the Koreans would beat him, so he fled to the south. There in the south, the Koreans didn't punish the pro-Japanese. It seems, down south, they wanted law and order above all else, and they kept the pro-Japanese Koreans in positions of power. The Japanese there even kept their weapons. It wasn't like that at all in the far north. When they heard about that, many Japanese sympathizers fled south.

Even I worried about my own safety. I fled from the town and went to my uncle.

Well, to keep the farms going, they needed skilled people, and I had worked a long time in agricultural technology. They needed someone who knew what he was doing with the water, and they said, "We'll forgive you. Come back." They kept sending messages and finally I went back.

YI CHAE'IM, (f) b. 1919, housewife, Kyŏnggi Province:
After liberation, I saw a Japanese mother in tattered clothes with a baby on her back, walking along the road. I really felt sorry for her. I also re-member the Japanese primary-school principal in Yangju county. He was killed by Koreans right after the war.

YANG SŎNGDŎK, (m) b. 1919, electrical engineer,
South Ch'ungch'ŏng Province, living in Shanghai:
There were about five hundred young Korean men in Shanghai at that time. Of those, only five were engineers, including me. We met in a the-ater. When we sang the Korean anthem tears streamed down our faces. We made Korean flags out of any paper we could find, and waved them furiously.

Change by Coercion

Koreans reacted to their sudden freedom with tears and laughter, guns and flags, confusion and hope. People, by long habit quiet and restrained, suddenly showed the depth of their confinement. Once they realized they were free, their emotions surged unrestrained, and things precious and long hidden burst into the open.

Women stood outside their doors, waving, hugging complete strangers, and offering festive food from hidden storage. Men waved Korean flags, freshly pulled from ingenious hiding places. One child passed a man standing alone on the dike of the river, lustily singing an unknown song. The child asked his aunt, "What song is that?" and the aunt replied softly, "He is singing our country's patriotic anthem."

Another person, remembering that day, seemed to speak for all Koreans. "I never talk about it," he said. "To talk is to remember—dare I remember? Even after all these years, I will see and hear it all again." His gaze became unfocused, he paused, and finally continued. "Surprise—joy—anticipation—fear—pathos—anger! All of them. All at once. I remember . . ." Tears began to slide from his eyes to his cheeks.

"I remember the bonfires," he said. "Many Shinto shrines quickly became objects of that anger. Crowds rushed up the steps, past the Torii gates, carrying axes and ropes. They tore down the wooden shrines, hacked them to pieces, and right there on the wide courtyards, they burned them to the ground."

Bonfires! What an appropriate way to help extinguish the gloom cast for over thirty-five years by the black umbrella of Japanese rule.

APPENDIX A: THE INTERVIEWS

Sex
   men: 36   women: 15

Birth Date
   1900–09: 7   1910–19: 28   1920–29: 19   1930–39: 6

Education by Type
   none: 9   village *sŏdang* schools: 14   Japanese: 25   Korean or mission: 10

Education by Level

	none	*sŏdang*	primary	high school	college
m:	5	4	14	9	4
f:	4	0	6	5	0

Jobs   (male only)
unskilled: 13   merchant or skilled: 14   professional: 9

Religion
Buddhist: 11   Christian: 18   None: 22

Birth Place by Province (listed from north to south)

Manchuria: 1	Kyŏnggi: 11
N. Hamgyŏng: 2	N. Ch'ungch'ŏng: 3
S. Hamgyŏng: 4	S. Ch'ungch'ŏng: 5
N. P'yŏngan: 3	N. Kyŏngsang: 5
S. P'yŏngan: 5	S. Kyŏngsang: 4
Hwanghae: 1	N. Chŏlla: 3
Kangwŏn: 3	S. Chŏlla: 1

APPENDIX B: BRINGING THE STORIES UP TO DATE
1945–1997

When we first collected these memories, we stopped the stories at 1945. Later, we returned to ask about their lives up to the present. We regret that there are no entries for people who either moved or died before we collected this information.

CHIN MYŎNGHŬI, with her mother and younger siblings, fled from the north during the Korean War. They walked to the south, but the mother got separated from the children and they never saw her again. Although Miss Chin was only eighteen at the time, she cared for her younger siblings, and later married and raised her own family. She joined her children in America.

CH'OE KILSŎNG became an elementary-school principal, but left teaching during the Korean War to go into business supplying salt to the army. Next, he opened a small shop in Seoul, which he continued to operate until retirement. After retirement he joined his children in California.

CH'OE P'ANBANG

CHŎNG CHAESU—See end of chapter 12.

CHŎNG KŬMJAE

CHŎNG T'AE'IK

CH'U PONGNYE's husband was a well-to-do businessman in Pusan, and during the Korean War he interpreted for the U.S. army. He passed away after the Korean War (1955), and she raised their seven children by herself. "It was a hard, hard life," she said. When some of the children emigrated to America, she joined them.

HONG ŬLSU—See end of chapter 3.

KANG PYŎNGJU—See end of chapter 5.

KANG SANG'UK fled from North Korea in 1947 and came to the United States as a university student in 1955, transferring from Seoul National University to the University of California, Berkeley, where he met his future wife. He moved to New York, worked as a research scientist, and later moved back to California to the Lawrence Livermore National Laboratory, where he continues to work. He has family in both America and Korea, and makes frequent trips back and forth.

KIM CHANDO—See end of chapter 7.

KIM HOJUN fled to South Korea in 1948 and became a policeman for eight years. He left the police force to go into business and did all right for the next twenty years. He had only one child, and came to America at the request of this child.

KIM P. [ANONYMOUS] (f) lived in Seoul. When the Korean War began, she lost everything and fled alone to her hometown near Pusan. She married a businessman who owned several textile factories. Their business went so well that they owned two automobiles complete with drivers. She and her husband came to America at the request of their children.

KIM P. [ANONYMOUS] (m) worked for a small township and worked actively in the young people's movement. He came to America in 1986, invited by his children.

KIM PONGSUK

KIM SAENGGWANG

KIM SANGSUN went into business selling tires and auto parts. He moved to America in 1980 to be with his children.

KIM SŎBUN

KIM SUNOK had a fruit stall in a large market and came to America in the 1970s.

KIM T. [ANONYMOUS] (m) worked in a factory all day, from six in the morning until 10 or 11 at night. He became an elder in the Christian church, and eventually came to America at the request of his children.

KIM WŎN'GŬK moved to South Korea during the Korean War and worked again for the Tobacco Authority, but he got a promotion and left the morphine section. He had six children, and moved to America to join them, where he served as president of the San Francisco Korean Senior Center.

KIM YŎSŎNG had many jobs. For several years he was the official photographer for school photos in Seoul. He also opened a crayon factory, then a window glass business. He did reasonably well in business, and when he retired, came to America to join his children.

PAE YŎNG'OK

PAK C. [anonymous] (f) moved to south Korea in 1947 and married in 1950 just before the Korean War started. Her husband was a textile merchant, who died in 1957. She never remarried, and raised her children alone. In 1989 she came to America to be with her daughter.

PAK CHUN'GI raised eight children while her husband handled a transportation business including forty trucks. They did well and bought a house in Seoul, but lost everything in the Korean War. Later they went into the printing and publishing business, and came to America in 1984 because several of their children were here.

PAK SŎNGP'IL recovered his three boats after liberation and stayed in the shipping business. He also owned many warehouses. For three years he dabbled in the stock market, and then started a taxi business, with taxis in both Pusan and Seoul. After he retired, he joined his children in America, where he served as president of the Santa Clara Korean Senior Center.

PAK TUYANG tried the wholesale liquor business and "just made enough" to get by. After retirement, he joined his children in America.

SIN KWANGSŎNG farmed all his life. He owned land in Andong and later moved to Chŏlla Province where he operated an orchard. "It was a hard life. After you paid tax, you had nothing left," he said. His children encouraged him to join them in America, which he did.

SONG SŎKCHI served as president of the East Bay Korean Senior Center.

U CH'AN'GU worked for the railway (Transportation Authority) and continued to do so until retirement. Then he joined his children in America.

YANG SŎNGDŎK, at liberation, immediately returned from Shanghai to South Korea. He married Yu Hyegyŏng. During the Korean War, all their assets were burned to the ground, including all documents and personal photos. After the war he tried fifteen different business ventures, and even tried to get into politics, running for election to the National Assembly. He decided to learn landscaping. One of his sons came to America, so when Mr. Yang was sixty-two, he came also. He planned to own a huge nursery, but found it took too much capital. He retired, and now helps in his son-in-law's landscaping business. In 1998 he became president of the East Bay Korean Senior Center.

YI CHAE'IM ran a small shop, selling all sorts of things. She came to America in the 1970s because her daughter worked at the Exchange Bank in the United States.

YI HAJŎN—See end of chapter 8.

YI OKHYŎN—See end of chapter 7.

YI OKPUN stayed home, took care of her household, and raised her children. "No complaints," she says. She came to America at the request of her children.

YI SANGDO continued to drive trucks until he retired, and then came to America at the request of his children.

YI SŬNGBONG

YU HYEGYŎNG—See end of chapter 10.

YU TŎKHŬI

APPENDIX C: HISTORICAL OVERVIEW

THE SCRAMBLE FOR POWER: 1850–1910

1854   Japan opened ports to western nations.

1858   China opened ports to western nations.

1876   Korea signed Kanghwa Treaty with Japan. Treaties followed with United States, Britain, France, Russia, and Germany, providing telegraph lines, telephone lines, electric streetcar systems, and other modern innovations.

1884   Protestant missionaries arrived from United States and Canada, built schools and hospitals.

1886   Methodist missionaries opened Ewha School for girls in Seoul.

1894   Japan declared war on China.

1895   Korean Queen Min assassinated.

1896   The *Independent* (*Tongnip Shinmun*), the first purely Korean-language newspaper was established.

1904   *Counselor Period*: Japan enforced a treaty with Korea so that Japan could give counsel to Korea for improvements in government administration; Russo-Japanese War.

1905   *Protectorate Agreement*: Japan proposed to protect the Korean monarch from "interference" by any third party and forbade Korea to enter into any treaty except through Japanese mediation.

1907   King Kojong forced to abdicate; Japanese opened the Royal Palace grounds as amusement park.

1907–1910
  Period of open rebellion. Active, armed struggle against the Japanese by formation of "Righteous Armies," guerrilla bands composed mainly of peasants and soldiers from the disbanded Korean army.

SUBJUGATION AND SUPPRESSION: 1910–1919

August 22, 1910
  Treaty of Annexation: Korea passed officially into the Japanese empire, and 518 years of Yi Dynasty rule ended.

1910   Police power given to Japanese. All Korean organizations placed under surveillance; 200,000 Koreans classified as "rebellious," and arrested for "suspicious behavior." Place names changed to Japanese pronunciation; for example, Korea became Chosen; Seoul became Keijo; and P'yŏngyang became Heijo. All commercial companies given Japanese managers. Governor-General ordered military and civilian police to raid bookstores and private homes to search and destroy books on Korean history. Land survey required all Korean landowners to register their land.

1911   Education Ordinance required all schools to teach and use Japanese, and controlled all textbooks. All officials, even schoolteachers, ordered to wear uniforms and carry swords.

1917   Japanese principals assigned to all schools. Grades 1–4 had Korean teachers; Grades 5–6 had Japanese teachers.

March 1, 1919

Independence Movement began.

APPEASEMENT AND CULTURAL ACCOMMODATION: 1920–1931

1920s   "Enlightened Administration": Military police system abandoned. Some businesses deregulated, making it easier for Koreans to become entrepreneurs.

1921   Some 330 Koreans appointed to government positions. Revised wages paid Koreans the same as Japanese on paper, but 60 percent a month bonus given to Japanese and not Korean. Japanese primary schools kept one Korean language class; all other subjects taught in Japanese. Korean publications and organizations allowed, but strict censorship maintained.

1925   Peace Preservation Law gave power to High Police
       Formation of first Korean Communist party.

1928   All teaching to be done in Japanese.

1929   Kwangju student uprising.

1930   Increased rice production exported to Japan.

ASSIMILATION: 1931–1945

By the end of the 1920s, Korea had been molded into a docile colony, linked to Japan by a trade cycle of exported raw materials and imported manufactured goods.

1931   Japanese established a puppet state of Manchukuo in Manchuria.

1937   *The War Years*: Government stressed importance of "guiding public opinion" and controlling the press. Japan began war on China. Japanese government began campaign to promote Japanese national spirit and erase Korean national identity. Government required recitation of the Imperial Oath and Pledge of the Imperial Subjects, and expanded role of High Police (thought control section).

1938   Korean language abolished in all public schools; Japanese language required for all public functions, including the securing of ration cards and public certification. Seven hundred fifty thousand youth "volunteers" mobilized to work in mines and factories. Price control and rationing enforced.

1940   Koreans required to change their names to Japanese. Population organized
       into Neighborhood Associations of ten-family units to monitor each other
       in all official instructions. Christians forced to work on Sundays; Shinto
       shrines placed in Christian churches.

1940–1944
       Thought police arrested five thousand "thought criminals."

1941   Classroom instruction curtailed; students required to join volunteer
       workforce.

1943   Military draft; all Korean cultural expression banned.

1945   A great massacre of Korean leaders was planned for mid August. "Some
       weeks after the atom bombs were dropped, we were told that over ten
       thousand leaders in Korean society who had been on the blacklist of the
       Japanese police were to have been arrested. In case of eventual Japanese
       defeat, the authorities thought these Koreans would become leaders and
       would retaliate against them. They had planned to massacre this group
       about the fifteenth of August, which proved to be the very day of the
       Japanese surrender."[1]

AUGUST 15, 1945: LIBERATION
       The Imperial Japanese colony came to an abrupt halt on August 15, 1945.
       Japan lost the war and, with it, its control of Korea.

NOTES

INTRODUCTION

1. Andrew C. Nahm, *Korea: Tradition and Transformation: A History of the Korean People* (Elizabeth, N.J.: Hollym, 1988), 142–43.

2. Ki-baik Lee, *A New History of Korea*, trans. Edward W. Wagner, with the assistance of Edward J. Shultz (Cambridge: Harvard University Press, 1984), 348.

3. Nahm, *Korea*, 238.

4. Nahm, *Korea*, 226.

5. Carter J. Eckert, *Offspring of Empire: The Koch'ang Kims and the Colonial Origins of Korean Capitalism, 1876–1945* (Seattle: University of Washington Press, 1991), xii.

6. Bruce Cumings, *Korea's Place in the Sun: A Modern History* (New York: Norton, 1997), 148.

7. Nahm, *Korea*, 229.

CHAPTER I. FIRST ENCOUNTERS

1. For many generations, people whose "free thoughts" ran counter to those of the ruling monarch found themselves exiled as far from the royal court as possible, usually to Cheju Island in the south or to the far northern provinces. Their descendents see this not as a dishonor, but as proof of their ancestors' strong independent spirit.

2. For explanation of *Kabo* Reforms, see Introduction, p. 1.

3. Patriotic Korean leaders felt the need to educate more Korean youths. Yi Sŭnghun, a businessman who owned a brassware manufacturing company, founded Osan School, a private secondary school for boys in Chŏngju, North P'yŏngan Province, in 1907. He then established a ceramics company and used the profits to support the school. Andrew C. Nahm, *Korea: Tradition and Transformation: A History of the Korean People* (Elizabeth, N.J.: Hollym, 1988), 213.

4. Nahm, *Korea*, 227.

5. For several hundred years Koreans had used land registers called *yang'an*, but these documents recorded only the size and productivity of plots. The kingdom had been plagued by boundary disputes and had been attempting to design a system to clarify boundaries and locations of individual plots. Edwin H. Gragert, *Landownership under Colonial Rule: Korea's Japanese Experience, 1900–1935* (Honolulu: University of Hawaii Press, 1994), 21.

6. Many Koreans shared this view of the Japanese land survey, but more recent studies find the "land grab" to be mainly general knowledge kept alive by rumor. Gi-Wook Shin, *Peasant Protest and Social Change in Colonial Korea* (Seattle: University of Washington Press, 1996), writes that, at least in specific cases, the Japanese did not radically alter Korean land tenure. In a group of over 9,000 land parcels, only 12 went unreported, less than 1 percent of the land was disputed during or after the survey, and except for land owned by palaces and government agencies, the survey brought little turnover of ownership. Gragert (*Landownership*, 137, 159) agrees and adds that "large land transfers began only with the massive economic dislocation caused by worldwide economic depression of 1930–1935."

7. Yi Tonghwi helped establish the first anti-Japanese organization in Manchuria, the Korean Revolutionary Corps (1915). He became Cabinet Minister of the Korean government in exile (1918), went to Shanghai, became premier of the Korean Provisional Government, and established the Korean Communist Party there in May 1920 (Nahm, *Korea*, 318).

CHANGE BY CHOICE

1. Ki-baik Lee, *A New History of Korea*, trans. Edward W. Wagner, with the assistance of Edward J. Shultz (Cambridge: Harvard University Press, 1984), 346.

2. Michael Edson Robinson, *Cultural Nationalism in Colonial Korea, 1920–1925* (Seattle: University of Washington Press, 1988), 4; Peter Duus, ed., *Cambridge History of Japan*, vol. 6, *The Twentieth Century* (Cambridge: Cambridge University Press, 1988), 236.

CHAPTER 2. SHOUTS OF INDEPENDENCE

1. Ki-baik Lee, *A New History of Korea*, trans. Edward W. Wagner, with the assistance of Edward J. Shultz (Cambridge: Harvard University Press, 1984), 344.

CHAPTER 4. CHOOSING AN EDUCATION

1. Andrew C. Nahm, *Korea: Tradition and Transformation: A History of the Korean People* (Elizabeth, N.J.: Hollym, 1988), 280; Stewart Lone and Gavan McCormack, *Korea since 1850* (New York: St. Martin's Press, 1993), 69.

2. Ramon H. Myers and Mark R. Peattie, eds., *The Japanese Colonial Empire, 1895–1945* (Princeton: Princeton University Press, 1984), 296.

3. Cho Mansik was a Christian-Nationalist leader who preached nonviolent resistance. At one time principal of Osan School in Chŏngju, he became a cabinet minister of the People's Republic of Korea in 1945. In 1946 the Soviets put him under house arrest (Nahm, *Korea*, 334).

CHAPTER 6. BUSINESS VENTURES AND ADVENTURES

1. Bruce Cumings, *Korea's Place in the Sun: A Modern History* (New York: Norton, 1997), 172.

CHAPTER 8. A RED LINE MARKS MY RECORD

1. Ham Sôkhôn, a Christian/Quaker educator and writer in the north, taught at Osan High School for ten years (1930–1940?) and was Education Chief in the temporary provincial government in 1945. In South Korea he was often arrested and beaten for antitotalitarian regime activities and was nominated for the Nobel Peace Prize in 1979 and 1985. He died in 1989.

2. Ahn Ch'angho founded Taesŏng private secondary school in P'yŏngyang in 1908. He promoted Korean national spirit through education and youth movements and was a leader of organized resistance to the Japanese in China, Manchuria, Siberia, and the United States. He died in a Korean prison in 1937.

CHAPTER 9. PASSIVE RESISTANCE

1. Gi-Wook Shin, *Peasant Protest and Social Change in Colonial Korea* (Seattle: University of Washington Press, 1996), 133.

2. Barrington Moore, *Injustice: The Social Bases of Obedience and Revolt* (New York: Sharpe, 1978), 156.

CHAPTER 11. BECOMING JAPANESE

1. Michael Robinson, "Forced Assimilation, Mobilization, and War," in *Korea: Old and New*, ed. Carter Eckert et al. (Seoul: Ilchokak, 1990), 315.

2. Andrew C. Nahm, *Korea: Tradition and Transformation: A History of the Korean People* (Elizabeth, N.J.: Hollym, 1988), 233, 255.

3. Wi Jo Kang, *Religion and Politics in Korea under the Japanese Rule* (Lewiston, N.Y.: Mellen Press, 1987), 39.

4. Gari Ledyard, Columbia University, New York, personal communication, March 1999.

APPENDIX C. HISTORICAL OVERVIEW

1. Wi Jo Kang, *Religion and Politics in Korea under the Japanese Rule* (Lewiston, N.Y.: Mellen Press, 1987), 43.

BIBLIOGRAPHY

Beasley, W. G. *Japanese Imperialism 1894–1945*. Oxford: Clarendon Press, 1987.

Bishop, Isabella. *Korea and Her Neighbors; A Narrative of Travel*. New York: Revell, 1897.

Cumings, Bruce. *Korea's Place in the Sun: A Modern History*. New York: Norton, 1997.

Deuchler, Martina. *Confucian Gentlemen and Barbarian Envoys: The Opening of Korea, 1875–1885*. Seattle: University of Washington Press, 1983.

Duus, Peter, ed. *Cambridge History of Japan*. Vol.6, *The Twentieth Century*. Cambridge: Cambridge University Press, 1988.

Eckert, Carter J. *Offspring of Empire: The Koch'ang Kims and the Colonial Origins of Korean Capitalism, 1876–1945*. Seattle: University of Washington Press, 1991.

Gragert, Edwin H. *Landownership under Colonial Rule: Korea's Japanese Experience, 1900–1935*. Honolulu: University of Hawaii Press, 1994.

Griffis, William Elliot. *Corea, The Hermit Nation*. New York: Charles Scribner's Sons, 1897.

Henderson, Gregory. *Korea: The Politics of the Vortex*. Cambridge: Harvard University Press, 1968.

Kang, Wi Jo. *Religion and Politics in Korea under the Japanese Rule*. Lewiston, N.Y.: Mellen Press, 1987.

Lee, Ki-baik. *A New History of Korea*. Translated by Edward W. Wagner, with the assistance of Edward J. Shultz. Cambridge: Harvard University Press, 1984.

Lone, Stewart, and Gavan McCormack. *Korea since 1850*. New York: St. Martin's Press, 1993.

McNamara, Dennis L. *The Colonial Origins of Korean Enterprise, 1910–1945*. Cambridge: Cambridge University Press, 1990.

Moore, Barrington. *Injustice: The Social Bases of Obedience and Revolt*. New York: Sharpe, 1978.

Myers, Ramon H., and Mark R. Peattie, eds. *The Japanese Colonial Empire, 1895–1945*. Princeton: Princeton University Press, 1984.

Nahm, Andrew C. *Korea: Tradition and Transformation: A History of the Korean People*. Elizabeth, N.J.: Hollym, 1988.

Robinson, Michael Edson. *Cultural Nationalism in Colonial Korea, 1920–1925*. Seattle: University of Washington Press, 1988.

Sands, William Franklin. *At the Court of Korea: Undiplomatic Memories*. 1892(?). Reprint, London: Century, 1987.

Shin, Gi-Wook. *Peasant Protest and Social Change in Colonial Korea*. Seattle: University of Washington Press, 1996.

Shin, Gi-Wook, and Michael Robinson, eds. *Colonial Modernity in Korea*. Cambridge: Harvard University Press, 2000.

INDEX OF PROPER NAMES

Hamamatsu, 127
Hangchow, 110
High Police, 85
Hiroshima, 139
Hokkaido Imperial University, 53
Holston Girls' High School, 33
Hong Kong, 36
Hong Ŭlsu, 3, 12, 15, 24–37
Hosei University, 87
Huch'ang, 56, 59
Hŭich'ŏn, 56, 60
Hwangju, 77, 80, 82

Ilchuk, 73
Indan mint pill, 107
Independence Army, 10
Independence Movement, 2, 4, 17–23, 54,
  88, 98
Independence, 107, 109
India, 36

Japanese names, 117–122
Japanese High Police, 35

Kabo Reforms, 1, 8
Kaech'ŏksa, 54
Kaesŏng, 33
Kang Chundal, 6
Kang Pyŏngju, 4–6, 15, 49–60
Kang Sang'uk, 40, 112, 115, 117, 133, 142
Kanggye, 59–60, 71, 112, 116
Kanggyŏng, 99
Kanto earthquake, 53
Kawasaki, 124
Keijo Medical College, 8
Kijang, 65
Kikuchi Kan, 45
Kim Chando, 75, 77–83
Kim Chongsŏ, 62
Kim Hangsik, 88
Kim Hojun, 39, 146
Kim Il Sŏng, 20, 49, 54, 83, 88
Kim Okgil, 89
Kim P. (anon., f), 45, 64, 116, 134, 145
Kim P. (anon., m), 118, 130
Kim Pongsuk, 134
Kim Saenggwang, 39

Kim Sangsun, 21, 67
Kim Sŏbun, 41–42, 44, 100, 136
Kim Sunok, 17, 62, 112
Kim T. (anon., m), 46
Kim Wŏn'gŭk, 11, 66, 114, 119, 132, 139
Kim Yŏsŏng, 20, 113
Kobe, 124, 127–128
Kongju, 95
Korea University, 83
Kŭm River, 99
Kwangju, 41, 47, 76, 101
Kwangsŏng High School, 87
Kyŏngsŏng, First High School, 52
Kyushu, 131

Lions' Club, 36

Manchus, 1
Manchukuo, 81, 85
Manchuria, 8, 13, 50, 71, 81–82, 85, 134
March First Movement, 21, 49. *See also*
  Independence Movement
Masan, 44
Meiji University, 87
Methodist, 138; American Southern, 33;
  Canadian, 75
Minami Jiro, 111
Misogi Harai, 58
Mitsubishi, 124
Mongol, 1
Monterey Language School, 98
Moore, Barrington, 99
Moriguchi, correspondent, 35
Morse Code, 69
Mulgŭm, 28, 60

Nagasaki, 131, 139
Nakano Police Station, 90
Nanam, 12
Nanking, 71
Neighborhood Association, 85, 101,
  133–134
Neighborhood Cell. *See* Neighborhood
  Association
New Year's Day, 116–117
New York, 60
North Korea, 20, 49, 54, 83

"One Body, One Spirit," 58
Osaka, 28, 34
Osan, 18, 50
Osan High School, 8, 49, 89

Pae Yŏng'ok, 137
Paehwa Middle School, 33
Pak C. (anon., f), 44, 64, 136
Pak Chun'gi, 21, 42, 102
Pak Myŏngyŏl, 22
Pak Sŏngp'il, 2, 22, 65, 117, 145
Pak Sunch'ŏn, 22
Pak Tuyang, 39
Pearl Harbor, 92
People's Reconstruction Committee, 98
Plant Analysis Bureau, 67
Pledge of Imperial Subjects, 115–116
Poland, 83
Pongsŏnhwa, 100
Presbyterian, 81, 102, 114
Presbyterian Theological Seminary, 75
Puch'ŏng-gun, 73
Pyŏkdong, 59–60, 143
Pyŏn Hiyŏng, 23
Pyŏn Yŏngt'ae, 23

Rhee Syngman, 23
Righteous Army, 99
Rotary Club, 36
Russia, 13, 27, 98, 132, 139, 145

Sach'on, 44
Saitama, 131
San Francisco, 83, 87
Sariwŏn, 97
Second P'yŏngyang High School, 89
Senzaki, 127
Shanghai, 89, 107, 109, 146
Shimonoseki, 28, 108, 110
Shinto, 58, 103, 111–115, 147
Shomeiji, 128
Siberia, 58
Sin Gwang Methodist Church, 103
Sin Kwangsŏng, 62, 102, 131
Singapore, 125
Sinp'ung, 60
Sinŭiju, 50, 56

Sokongduk Primary School, 74
Song Sŏkchi, 72, 114, 133
Sŏngjin, 141
South East Asia, 36
South Seas, 66
Spiritual Training and Exercise, 58
Sunch'ŏn, 22
Sung'in Business High School, 87
Sungin Commercial High School, 46
Suwŏn, 77
Suwŏn Agricultural College, 54, 77

Taedong Police Station, 90
Taegu, 35, 70
Taisho, Emperor, 93
Teishintai. *See* Comfort women
Terauchi Masatake, 11
Thirty-Sixers, 34
Tobacco Authority, 66
Tojo Hideki, 36
Tokyo, 22–23, 29, 87, 90, 110, 115
Tokyo Nichi Nichi Shinbun, 4
Tonghak, 1, 10
Tuman River, 56

U Ch'an'gu, 47, 103
Uchiyama Bookstore, 109
Ŭijŏngbu, 73
Ulsan, 129
Underwood, Dr., 46
Ungjin High School, 81
United States, 27, 31, 33, 132, 139; Army of,
    36
University of California, Berkeley, 98

Volunteer Service Brigade. *See* Comfort
    women

Waesŏk, 24
Wilson, Woodrow, 14
Women's Association, 135
Women's Service Corps, 110
Wŏnju, 144
Wŏnsan, 75–76, 80, 137, 145
Wŏnsan Girls' High School, 75
World War II, 95, 130, 142

ABOUT THE AUTHOR

Hildi Kang, a graduate of University of California, Berkeley,
is the eldest daughter-in-law in a large Korean family.
Her lifetime interest in Korean history has resulted in
journal articles, historical fiction for children, and invitations
as guest lecturer in Korean Studies programs.